We Believe in God and in Christ. Not in the Church

We Believe in God and in Christ. Not in the Church

The Influence of Wessel Gansfort on Martin Bucer

MARIJN DE KROON
TRANSLATED BY MARIA SHERWOOD SMITH

*Princeton Theological Seminary Studies
in Reformed Theology and History*

WJK WESTMINSTER
JOHN KNOX PRESS
LOUISVILLE · KENTUCKY

© 2009 Marijn de Kroon

Originally published as *"Wij geloven in God en in Christus. Niet in de kerk"* by Marijn de Kroon and published by Uitgeverij Kok Kampen. © Utigeverij Kok Kampen, 2004

First English edition
Published by Westminster John Knox Press
Louisville, Kentucky

09 10 11 12 13 14 15 16 17 18—10 9 8 7 6 5 4 3 2 1

Scripture quotations, unless otherwise indicated, are from the New Revised Standard Version of the Bible, copyright © 1989 by the Division of Christian Education of the National Council of the Churches of Christ in the U.S.A., and used by permission.

Book design by Sharon Adams
Cover design by Jennifer K. Cox

Library of Congress Cataloging-in-Publication Data

Kroon, Marijn de
    [Wij geloven in God en in Christus, niet in de kerk. English]
    We believe in God and in Christ, not in the church / Marijn de Kroon ; translated by Maria Sherwood Smith.—1st English ed.
        p. cm.—(Princeton theological seminary studies in Reformed theology and history)
    Includes bibliographical references (p.   ) and index.
    ISBN 978-0-664-23293-1 (alk. paper)
    1. Church—Authority—History of doctrines.   2. Reformation.   3. Bucer, Martin, 1491–1551.   4. Gansfort, Wessel, 1419–1489.   5. Augustine, Saint, Bishop of Hippo.   I. Title.
    BT91.K7613   2009
    262'.8—dc22   2009006571

PRINTED IN THE UNITED STATES OF AMERICA

♾ The paper used in this publication meets the minimum requirements of the American National Standard for Information Sciences—Permanence of Paper for Printed Library Materials, ANSI Z39.48-1992

Westminster John Knox Press advocates the responsible use of our natural resources. The text paper of this book is made from 30 percent post-consumer waste.

"We Believe in God and in Christ. Not in the Church"
Wessel Gansfort (d. 1489) and Martin Bucer (d. 1551).
A Dictum by Augustine and a Writing by Wessel Gansfort
on Authority in the Church,
Translated into English and Set in Context
with Reference to the Sources.

Contents

Contents

Editor's Preface

An attentive and knowledgeable scholar can find all kinds of fascinating surprises in the course of editing the writings of a learned predecessor. That is what Dr. de Kroon has done for Martin Bucer. In the process, he has also uncovered an intriguing and rich dimension of the relationship between the interpretation of Augustine in the late Middle Ages and its use in the Protestant Reformation.

The story began when Dr. de Kroon was editing Bucer's commentary on Romans. In his remarks on Romans 8:18 about the renewal of the whole creation, Bucer cites with approval Wessel Gansfort, the late medieval Dutch theologian called "the light from the Low Countries." Although the reformer speaks of Wessel Gansfort in his correspondence, this citation in Romans is the only instance in Bucer's published writings. Dr. de Kroon began to explore the relationship between Bucer and Wessel Gansfort. One remarkable discovery focused on the use by these two theologians of Augustine's most controversial statement relating Scripture to the authority of the church; their "take" on this dictum provides the title of this book. The distinctive antithetical formulation and critique of Augustine's words that Wessel Gansfort uses turns up in Bucer's writings—which are otherwise characterized by a very different and prolix style. What is going on here?

The major portion of this book explores the history of interpretation of Augustine's statement from the middle of the fourteenth century to the end of the fifteenth and then its appropriation by Bucer. What makes this presentation unusual is the fact that the reader is invited along to make the journey through the sources, as each of the seven medieval theologians reflects on Augustine's famous words. The longest text translated is Wessel Gansfort's treatise on authority in the church.

The book's organization is essentially chronological. The introduction discusses Augustine's statement in its historical context. Chapter 1 then provides translations of excerpts from the writings of six theologians, from William of Occam (d. 1347) to Gabriel Biel (d. 1495), commenting on Augustine's dictum. Chapter 2 presents in a new translation the full text of Wessel Gansfort's treatise *Ecclesiastical Dignity and Power: True and Right Obedience*, in which Augustine's famous statement serves as the "backbone." Chapter 3 then explores the relationship between Wessel Gansfort and Martin Bucer, including the explicit citation in the reformer's commentary on Romans 8:18 and the anonymous references in various citations of Augustine's dictum, as well as further evidence for Bucer's knowledge of Wessel Gansfort and similarities between the two.

Professor de Kroon's book in the original Dutch and Latin received an award from the Netherlands Organization for Scientific Research. We are very happy to be able to present to a wider audience this fascinating view of one way that the young Reformed tradition identified and built on the creative thinking of earlier theologians . . . a presentation which may also challenge modern readers to continue exploring vital questions of authority in a very different world. We thank Professor de Kroon for contributing his book to our series and Mr. Yoshiyuki Kato for making the indexes.

Author's Preface
for the English Translation

MARIJN DE KROON

Martin Bucer's correspondence contains enthusiastic praise for Wessel Gans-fort of Groningen, but I know of only one instance in his writings for pub-lication in which Bucer, one of the leading lights of the Reformation, refers to the "light of the world from the Low Countries." The reference occurs in Bucer's magnum opus, his lengthy and erudite commentary on the Epistle to the Romans, published in 1536. Chapter 3 of this book will discuss this chance occurrence in more detail.

But Bucer's sudden allusion to Wessel's works is intriguing. It seems accu-rate, and gives the impression that the Strasbourg reformer is familiar with the works of his fellow theologian from Groningen. The allusion merits fur-ther investigation.

The first great surprise to emerge is that the proverbial expression chosen as the title of this book, which turns up in numerous variants in Bucer's oeuvre, in fact originates with Wessel Gansfort, was inspired by him, and was even for-mulated by him. Secondly, this antithetical phrase shows the critical response of both theologians to Augustine's famous saying: "I would not believe the gospel, were it not that the authority of the Catholic church compels me to do so."

Two statements, three leading roles! The dictum of the church father spans an entire millennium. The introduction to the current volume explores the meaning of Augustine's phrase. Wessel Gansfort takes the laurels for the fact that he went further than all others in interpreting Augustine's words as a critical comment on the church.

To provide the reader with a more differentiated backdrop, chapter 1 briefly outlines the history of the reception of this famous statement in the late Middle Ages and how it was interpreted by a series of theologians of renown. In part due to this approach, the investigation of sources became a major component of the current study.

Wessel's exposé on the subject of authority in the church is published here in a modern English translation, presented as a critical edition with explanatory notes (chapter 2). What is revolutionary about this exposé is that the Scriptures themselves are the source. The Dutch theologian views the exercise of authority within the church as a reciprocal matter, a contract between two parties, like an agreement between doctor and patient, entered into "of their own free will and from the heart." This vision of Wessel Gansfort's makes the treatise a fascinating document, a significant contribution to Dutch theological literature. Wessel questions the hierarchically structured, authoritarian manner in which authority is implemented in the church, and the issues he raises are still highly relevant today. *Tolle lege!*

ACKNOWLEDGMENTS

On the publication of the English translation of this work, my thanks go out, first and foremost, to Professor Elsie McKee. I am convinced that it is entirely thanks to her stamina, and especially her deep theological understanding, that this book has seen the light of day, and I am grateful to her for including the work in Princeton Theological Seminary's series Studies in Reformed Theology and History, of which she is the academic editor. In addition, I would like to thank her sincerely for what she modestly refers to as "a little editing": a few clarifying passages inserted into chapter 1 to provide better insight into the theological movements of the late Middle Ages, which are thus made more accessible, particularly for students.

A sincere thank-you is due also to Dr. Donald K. McKim, for welcoming me so kindly into the circle of authors published by the Westminster John Knox Press.

I would like to express my warm thanks to the translator of this work, Dr. Maria Sherwood-Smith, who—with great skill and perseverance—shared with me the joys and burdens of bringing this English translation into the world. Perseverance was called for especially when it came to translating chapter 2, which she took to calling "the Killer Chapter." I am eternally grateful to her for her work.

This translation was made possible by the financial support of the Netherlands Organization for Scientific Research (NWO). I am grateful to the

NWO for their assistance and thank Ms. Winfred Geldof of NWO for her friendly and efficient help.

I dedicate this book to the memory of Cornelis Augustijn (d. January 1, 2008). My memories of our shared work, of his lucid advice time and time again over many years, and above all of the depth of his friendship constitute an infinitely precious inheritance.

Introduction

A strange turn of events: The words of a church father, who was not even remotely in sight when I first embarked on this study, are now the focus of the introduction and form a recurring motif throughout. The surprising turn this research took was that the statement of Augustine quoted below—from his letter to the Manicheans, *Contra epistulam Manichaei quam vocant fundamenti (Epistula fundamenti)*—rather unexpectedly forced its way to center stage.[1]

For this study all began, not with Augustine, but with Martin Bucer. The link is a curious one. It lies in Bucer's commentary on Romans 8:18, where—in the only explicit instance I have found in his oeuvre—the commentator refers to a certain Wessel Gansfort, a theologian from Groningen, in the Netherlands. I discuss this matter in more detail in chapter 3.[2] And so the quest through the works of this "light from the Low Countries" begins.[3]

1. AUGUSTINE MAKES HIS ENTRANCE

For anyone interested in the history of Western Christianity, Augustine is virtually impossible to avoid. Sooner or later, one is bound to come across the

1. Augustine, *Contra epistulam Manichaei quam vocant fundamenti liber unus Epistula fundamenti*, 5,6; MSL 42:176; CSEL 25:1, 197s.
2. See chapter 3, introduction.
3. As stated on the title page of Wessel's *Opera*: *Qui olim LVX MVNDI vulgo dictus est.*

famous bishop of Hippo. As the great Augustine expert A. Damasus Trapp put it, the influence of this church father was *"verheerend gross"* ("overwhelmingly great"). So great was this influence—as Damasus Trapp intimated to me during his time at the University of Tübingen, Germany—that it was not necessarily always a blessing. Does this reservation hold true, perhaps, for the famous saying of Augustine's that surfaced in the course of my search for interfaces between Wessel Gansfort and Martin Bucer: "I would not believe the gospel, were it not that the authority of the church compels me to do so"?[4]

It would be overly hasty for me to draw this conclusion on the basis of my research thus far into the reception of Augustine in the late Middle Ages. My examination of six representative theologians' interpretations of Augustine's dictum, presented in translation and with commentary in chapter 1, constitutes too meager a basis for such a statement. The period spanned by these theologians—the 150 years between William of Occam and Gabriel Biel—is also too limited. From the very start, however, the intention behind my "brief reception history" was much more modest. Its central purpose is to provide a deeper perspective from which to view Wessel Gansfort's interpretation of Augustine's words, to fill in the background against which the individual, even willful nature of this interpretation stands out.

Wessel's independence of mind is evident immediately in his discussion with Jakob Hoeck of Naaldwijk, and is even more striking in the treatise *Ecclesiastical Dignity and Power*, which is presented in a full translation in chapter 2.[5] In this treatise, Wessel is no longer content to put the authority of the church in its place in general, abstract terms—that is, *below* the Gospels, and *below* God. Rather, his criticism is directed in concrete terms toward those who hold authority within the church: the pope, prelates, *pastores*, and *doctores*. These are the figures he puts firmly in their place, whom he relegates mercilessly to their position. Wessel gives full rein to the train of thought that characterizes his interpretation of Augustine's words. The Dutch theologian formulates his thoughts sharply and combatively and shows a marked preference for paradoxes. He is the *magister contradictionum*.[6]

---

4. MSL 42:176.

5. See chap. 2, section 5.

6. This is how Jacob Hoeck characterizes Wessel Gansfort. (See chap. 2.1, n. 4.) The same description also occurs in the *Vita* of Wessel Gansfort by Albert Hardenberg; *Opera* ** 3 [a].

2. THROUGH THE BACK DOOR OF CANON LAW
(*CORPUS IURIS CANONICI*)

William of Occam not only marks the beginning of a new school of theological thought, nominalism, but also sets the tone for all late medieval commentaries on Augustine's statement,[7] as an overview of these interpretations shows (chapter 1). The most striking in this respect is the interpretation of Gabriel Biel, the last in the series in chronological terms. In his *Canonis misse Expositio*, he quotes Occam verbatim (though without referring to his illustrious predecessor, the *venerabilis inceptor*, by name).[8]

William of Occam quotes the dictum in question from Augustine's response to the *Epistula fundamenti* twice in his *Dialogus*.[9] On both occasions, he cites his source as the *Corpus Iuris Canonici*, more particularly the canon *Palam*, which forms part of *Distinctio XI* of the first book of the *Decretum Gratiani*.[10] In actual fact, William is quoting a gloss, a supplementary annotation to the canon of ecclesiastical law. Canon law provides an opening to introduce the church father's authority into the proceedings, giving his words particular weight or gravitas from the very start.

A quotation from Augustine underpinning a tenet of canon law! This typifies the powerful position ecclesiastical lawyers held in the papal curia; they interpreted Augustine's statement above all as a firm endorsement of the authority of the church, and of the pope's jurisdiction in particular. Although this matter is beyond the scope of the current research, it seems to me eminently possible that when the *Corpus Iuris Canonici* became established about 1150, Augustine's statement entered the corpus by way of one of the existing *Florilegia*.

However, even before this collection of the precepts of ecclesiastical law was edited, the influence of legal thought was irrepressibly on the advance in

7. See chap. 1, section 1.
8. See chap. 1, section 6.
9. Guillemus de Occam, *Dialogus de potestate papae et imperatoris. Compendium errorum Johannis XXII* (Turin, 1959; reprint of the edition published in Frankfurt in 1614), 402 and 864.
10. *Corpus Iuris Canonici* (CIC), *Decretum Gratiani*, D. XI, c. *Palam*. Augustine is cited in the commentary to this canon: . . . *in libro contra epist*[ulam] *Fundamenti*. . . However, the text of this canon is actually taken—with very few deviations—from Augustine's treatise *Contra Faustum Manichaeum* I. 11, c. II; MSL 42:246. In the edition of the *Corpus* that I used (Antwerp, 1648), the commentary is printed immediately below the text; in the standard edition by A. Friedberg (Leipzig, 1879), the allusion to the *Epistula fundamenti* is relegated to a footnote.

the Western church. As Bernard of Clairvaux put it, "The curia is buzzing with laws, but they are those of Justinian rather than of the Lord."[11]

In his *Dialogus*, written almost 200 years later, William of Occam tries to turn back the tide, and he is not without success. But even he cannot quite break with the interpretation of Augustine's statement that is favorable to the authorities. Yet this is just what Wessel Gansfort does do, and in a particularly radical manner at that. Hence the significance of his interpretation of Augustine's words in the latter's response to the *Epistula fundamenti*.

3. AUGUSTINE'S CRITICISM
OF MANI'S *EPISTULA FUNDAMENTI*

Augustine was a Manichean, a follower of Mani, for at least nine years (373–382).[12] Later, having become a Catholic bishop, he devoted thirty works to opposing the Manichean heresy. Modern research into Augustine places great value on the church father's gnostic past, and views its influence—on the *Confessions*, for example—as a positive factor, an asset.

We find traces of Augustine's anti-Manichean stance in the text fragment that is at the center of interest here, which occurs in Augustine's response to Mani's manifesto. I limit myself to a critical reading of chapters 4 and 5 of Augustine's criticism of Mani's *Epistula fundamenti*, which provide the immediate context for Augustine's words: "I would not believe the gospel . . ."[13] I am firmly convinced that the controversy with the Manicheans is vital for a balanced interpretation of this famous dictum.

Introduction

Chapter 4 of Augustine's response to the Manichean manifesto forms the introduction to his attack. From a literary point of view, the chapter is a concise but sophisticated argument—with slightly triumphalist overtones—in which the skilled rhetorician denigrates his former cobelievers (who are still

---

11. "Et quidem quotidie perstrepunt in palatio leges, sed Justiniani, non Domini." Bernard of Clairvaux, *De Consideratione* 1, 4; MSL 182:732.

12. J. van Oort, *Mani, Manichaeism and Augustine: The Rediscovery of Manichaeism and Its Influence on Western Christianity* (Tbilisi, 1998), 39–53. Idem, *Augustinus' Confessiones. Gnostische en christelijke spiritualiteit in een diepzinnig document* (Turnhout, 2002). Cf. also TRE 22:25–45 (Alexander Böhlig, *Manichäismus*).

13. MSL 42:175–76. For a text-critical analysis of the Manichean manifesto, see E. Feldmann, *Die 'Epistula Fundamenti' der nordafrikanischen Manichäer. Versuch einer Rekonstruktion* (Altenberge, 1987; Lit. Verzeichnis), 135–52.

his townspeople, his neighbors, so to speak).[14] We see this strategy at its most effective as he sneers:

> And I shall not even begin to speak of that sincere wisdom of yours, since—as you believe—it is not to be found in the Catholic Church anyway. It is only a few, spiritual people [i.e., the Manicheans], who can aspire to such wisdom in this life.[15]

Augustine also pokes fun at the Manicheans' constant talk of truth:

> I admit we are a bit sluggish in intelligence, and we have many short-comings in our lives, so that there is not too much to be seen of all that truth. But in your circles—where there is no longer anything that might attract or keep me—one hears only hollow promises of truth.
> . . . For where so much is promised but never shown, nobody shall move me from that faith that binds my soul to the Christian faith with so many strong ties.[16]

Augustine then lists a series of factors that bind him to the Catholic Church. It is an impressive list, but nevertheless one that appeals strongly to external forms of authority and prestige. At this point he does not enter into matters of content.

> What binds me [to the Catholic Church] is the consensus of nations and of peoples. I am bound by authority founded in miracles, nour-ished by hope, augmented by love, confirmed by antiquity. I am bound by the succession of priests, beginning at the very seat of the apostle Peter . . . right up to the present episcopate. And I am bound, finally, by the name "Catholic [Church]" itself. It is not without cause that the church has managed to retain sole possession of this name among so many heresies. [In conclusion, Augustine even lists churches and buildings that belong to the Catholic Church.][17]

14. F. van der Meer, *Augustinus de zielzorger. Een studie over de praktijk van een kerk-vader* (Utrecht, Brussels, 2nd ed., 1949), 136f.
15. MSL 42:175. (ut omittam sincerissimam sapientiam, quam in Ecclesia esse catholica non creditis, ad cujus cognitionem pauci spirituales in hac vita perveniunt).
16. Ibid. (. . . etiamsi propter nostrae intelligentiae tarditatem vel vitae meritum veritas nondum se apertissime ostendat. Apud vos autem, ubi nihil horum est quod me invitet ac teneat, sola personat veritatis pollicitatio . . . si autem tantummodo promit-titur, et non exhibetur, nemo me movebit ab ea fide quae animum meum tot et tantis nexibus christianae religioni astringit).
17. Ibid. (tenet consensio populorum atque gentium: tenet auctoritas miraculis inchoata, spe nutrita, charitate aucta, vetustate firmata: tenet ab ipsa sede Petri apos-toli . . . usque ad praesentem episcopatum successio sacerdotum: tenet postremo ipsum Catholicae nomen, quod non sine causa inter tam multas haereses sic ista Ecclesia sola obtinuit).

Interpretation

The tone is set, the tendency established. By way of a conclusion to this introduction, and to pave the way to chapter 1, I would like to present an interpretation of Augustine's statement from the point of view of its immediate
context in his oeuvre (chap. 5).

The Manichean manifesto refers to Mani as "the apostle of Jesus Christ,
through the providence of God the Father."[18] It is characteristic of Augustine, in a positive sense, that he does not reject this pretentious statement out
of hand. The apostle of Jesus Christ? The Scriptures speak of Paul in these
terms,[19] but they do not mention a Mani. No, Augustine's approach is more
subtle. He does not wish to irritate his former cobelievers unnecessarily:

> Patience, I pray you, and pay attention to my point. I do not believe
> that he [Mani] is an apostle of Christ. Now, I beg you, do not become
> incensed and start to curse.[20]

What the Manichaeans need to do, he says, is come up with better arguments:

> For you [Mani] promised me knowledge of the truth, and yet now you
> are forcing me to believe something I know nothing about. Perhaps
> you will read me the Gospel and will try to derive the credibility of
> the person of Mani from it. . . . Imagine you met someone who did
> not yet believe the gospel. What would you do if he said, "I do not
> believe"? Yet I myself would not believe the gospel were it not that
> the authority of the Catholic Church moves me to do so.[21]

> Do you really think that I am so stupid that I would believe whatever
> you wished and disbelieve whatever you wished, all without any rea-
> son being given? . . . Perhaps if you could find something in the gospel
> about the Manichean apostolate that was incontrovertibly clear, then
> you might weaken the authority of the Catholic Church for me . . .
> Then I might no longer be able to believe in the gospel.[22]

18. *Manichaeus apostolus Jesu Christi providentia Dei Patris* (Op. cit., 176).
19. 1 Cor. 1:1: "Paul, called to be an apostle of Christ Jesus by the will of God."
20. MSL 42:176 (Jam cum bona patientia, si placet, attendite quid quaeram. Non
credo istum esse apostolum Christi. Quaeso ne succenseatis, et maledicere incipiatis).
21. Ibid. (. . . promittebas enim scientiam veritatis, et nunc quod nescio cogis ut
credam. Evangelium mihi fortasse lecturus es, et inde Manichaei personam tentabis
asserere. Si ergo invenires aliquem, qui Evangelio nondum credit, quid faceres dicenti
tibi, Non credo? Ego vero Evangelio non crederem, nisi me catholicae Ecclesiae commoveret auctoritas).
22. Ibid. (usque adeo me stultum putas, ut nulla reddita ratione quod vis credam,
quod non vis non credam? . . . Quod si forte in Evangelio aliquid apertissimum de
Manichaei apostolatu invenire potueris, infirmabis mihi Catholicorum auctoritatem . . . jam nec Evangelio credere potero . . .).

This reveals the true reason why Augustine sets so much store by the authority of the Catholic Church: It is because the gospel is so dear to him.

> For this reason, if there is nothing to be found in the gospel about the apostolate of Mani that is completely new, I would rather believe the Catholics than you.[23]

4. INTRODUCTORY NOTE TO CHAPTER 1

I have deliberately kept my own interpretation of Augustine's dictum to a minimum, in order to focus all the reader's attention on the sources themselves. I provide the documents in translation to ensure that they are as accessible as possible. The Latin text is quoted in full in the notes.

The commentaries on Augustine's statement by seven renowned theologians are crying out to be studied in more detail. Scholars will want to get their teeth into these texts; but interested laypeople too will find much food for thought and debate. And this is due, in the final instance, to Augustine's words themselves. They raise issues that seem, time and time again, to elude a satisfactory answer. For the church father writing so many centuries ago voices questions about the relationship between the gospel and the church that are still immensely relevant today.

---

23. Ibid. (Quapropter si nihil manifestum de Manichaei apostolatu in Evangelio reperitur, Catholicis potius credam quam tibi). Cf. J. van Oort, *Mani*, 46: "His emphasis on the truth of the Scriptures can also be explained as a reaction to Manichaean criticism."

1

Six Interpretations

"I would not believe the gospel . . ."
(Augustine)

The life of Augustine's dictum in the later Middle Ages can be traced through significant citations of it by seven of the most important theologians of this period in western Europe. Six voices are presented in this chapter, and Wessel Gansfort's considerably longer text forms the next chapter. All six sections here are organized in similar fashion, beginning with a brief introduction to the theologian. The extract from his writings that uses Augustine's words forms the central text. This is followed by the modern author's commentary on the way the medieval writer interprets (and applies) the church father's dictum. The original Latin text is given at the end of each section.

1. WILLIAM OF OCCAM (d. 1347)

The first text to be examined here is by William of Occam, known as the *venerabilis inceptor*, who introduced a new mode of theological thinking in the late Middle Ages, nominalism. Nominalism denies the truth value of general terms *(universalia)* and accords greater value to the logical analysis of the words *(nomina)* that we form, the terms *(termini)* in which we make judgments, and the concepts *(conceptus)* in which we summarize our thoughts. The gnoseology (theory of knowledge) of this new way of thinking *(via moderna)* is characterized by a skeptical approach, precisely when it comes to the knowledge of

God. Instead, in this theology, God's free will and beneficence play a promi-
nent role.

Occam's "way" stands at the very beginning of what is known as the "controversy of the ways," which is so strong an influence on the theological landscape in the late Middle Ages. The matter of the *universalia* is complicated
still further by the fact that the realists' way *(the via antiqua)* in this theological controversy is further subdivided into various branches: Albertism (after
Albertus Magnus, d. 1280), Thomism (after Thomas Aquinas, d. 1274), and
Scotism (after Duns Scotus, d. 1308).[1] I am aware that this explanation of
the "controversy of the ways" is all too brief and unsatisfying, but I believe
Occam's interpretation of Augustine's statement is all the more striking
because of this controversy.

Text

402, 37–54 . . . Sometimes the word "church" may mean not only the whole
congregation of all Catholics who are still alive, but also all the faithful
departed. It is in this latter sense that Augustine understands the word in
his book *Contra Manichaeos*, which is quoted in *Distinctio XI*, in the canon
Palam, which states: "It is clear that in cases of doubt about faith and certainty
about faith, the authority of the Catholic Church must have the last word.
This authority is confirmed from the firmest foundations of the seats of the
apostles themselves right up to the present day, in the long series of bishops
who have succeeded them and through the consent and assertion of so many
peoples."[2] Here the "Catholic Church" refers to the bishops and the peoples
who have succeeded one another from the days of the apostles right up to the
present day.

And it is in this sense that Augustine understands the term "church" where
he asserts: "I would not believe the gospel were it not that the authority of the
church compels me."

For "church" in this sense includes the authors of the gospel and all the
apostles, as has been shown. Therefore the authoritative words of Augustine—if understood correctly—cannot be taken to mean that the pope, who
drew up the ecclesiastical laws, is more to be believed than is the gospel. Con-

1. For the theological schools of thought mentioned here, please see the relevant
specialist literature. For a general introduction to William of Occam, see TRE 25:6–
18: *I Ockham, II Ockhamismus* Lit. 17–18 (Gordon Leff, Volker Leppin). See also chap.
3 below: Concluding remarks (A) and n. 113.
2. *Dialogus* (see introduction, n. 9) 402:41–43 = *Decretum Gratiani* D.XI, c. *Palam*.
In the gloss below the main text, Augustine's *Liber contra epistulam Fundamenti* is
adduced in confirmation of this canon. Cf. introduction, n. 10.

sequently, it is impossible to prove that we should place more faith in the sacred tenets of ecclesiastical law than in the holy gospel.

However, it must be conceded that the *church*, which is the multitude of all Catholics who have ever been, from the days of the prophets and apostles to our own days, is more greatly to be believed than is the gospel. Not because the gospel is to be doubted in any way whatsoever, but because the sum is greater than the parts.

Thus the church that has greater authority than the evangelist is that church of which the author of the gospel is discerned as being part.

Commentary

Whose task is it to decide who is a heretic and who is orthodox? Is it the task of an expert in canon law, or of a theologian? This question, Occam says, has become a matter of dissent in Christendom. This is how he opens his famous work the *Dialogus*.[3] Should it perhaps be the experts in canon law? he asks. For after all, do not the origins of canon law lie in the church, rather than in the gospel? This would seem to suggest that the experts in this field are right in claiming for themselves Augustine's statement that "I would not believe the gospel, were it not that the authority of the church compels me." The pope is the true founder of canon law in any case, Occam adds. For is it not he who determines the symbols and articles of the faith . . . ?[4]

Perhaps this may sound convincing, but not for William of Occam. For him, theology is far superior to the science of canon law. "Theology is the science of the sacred Scripture." "God himself is the direct founder of this science, and all our faith derives from him."[5]

In his *Dialogus*, William of Occam can scarcely repress his aversion to the curialists, the legal scholars of the papal curia. It is precisely these canonists who try to extend the power of the pope too far—even in purely secular matters—underpinning their stance with legal arguments. No doubt the Englishman Occam's aversion had been strengthened when he was called to account for his theological views before Pope John XXII in Avignon in 1324–28. The second part of the *Dialogus* is a head-on attack on this pope, especially on his stance in the shameful dispute about the evangelical ideal of poverty. In this conflict, Occam sided with Michael of Cesena, general of the Franciscan

3. *Dialogus* 399:29.
4. The pope would seem to be the appropriate person to answer the question posed, since the activities of *symbolum fidei ordinare* and *articulos fidei rite diffinire* both fall within his power. He is also the *auctor . . . scientiae canonistarum*; ibid., 52–54.
5. *Scientia scripturae divinae, quae theologia vocatur*; op. cit., 400:57. *auctor immediatus Deus est, a quo est tota fides nostra*; ibid., 65.

order, and fled with him from Avignon to take refuge at the court of Louis IV
of Bavaria, near Munich. He wrote his *Dialogus* during this period.[6]

Is it then primarily the task of the theologian to determine whether someone is heretical or orthodox in his beliefs? This is perhaps the view that we
might expect, Occam himself being a theologian. But his answer is surprising.
In fact, he does not side with either party. His choice rests on the church, but
not the church of the lawyers, and equally not that of the theologians, but
rather the church in the most general sense of the word: the universal church.
He even goes so far as to posit that *this* church also comprises the gospel, that
the gospel is part of this church! At the same time, he is firm that one can
admit no doubts where the gospel is concerned, no doubts whatsoever.

Augustine's words set William of Occam thinking about the church, and
his own words, in turn, were a challenge that provided food for thought for
many others.

Latin Text

From Guillemus de Occam, *Dialogus de potestate papae et imperatoris.
Compendium errorum Johannis XXII* (Turin, 1959; reprint of the edition
published in Frankfurt in 1614), lib. I, cap. IV, 402, 37–54.

402, 37–54 . . . Aliquando vero nomen *Ecclesiae* non solum totam congrega-
tionem catholicorum viventium, sed etiam fideles mortuos comprehendit.

Et isto modo ultimo accipit Augustinus in *libro contra Manicheos* et recitatur
2 [=XI] *di*[stinctio] *c*[anon] *palam*. Qui ait: *palam est quantum in re dubia ad fidem
et certitudinem valeat catholicae ecclesiae auctoritas, quae ab ipsis fundatissimis sedibus apostolorum, usque ad hodiernum diem succedentibus sibimet episcoporum serie et
tot populorum concessione* [sic!] *et assertione firmatur.* Ubi ecclesia catholica episcopos et populos a tempore apostolorum usque ad hodiernum diem sibimet
succedentes importat.

Et sic accipit nomen *Ecclesiae* Augustinus cum asserit, quod *non crederet
evangelium, nisi eum auctoritas ecclesiae compelleret.* Ista enim ecclesia scriptores
evangelii et omnes apostolos comprehendit, sicut probatum est. Quare ex
auctoritate Augustini sane intellecta inferri non potest, quod magis sit credendum summo pontifici canonum conditori quam evangelio.

Et per consequens probari non potest, quod maior fides exhibenda sit sacris
canonibus quam evangelio sancto. Conceditur tamen, quod magis credendum
est *ecclesiae*, quae est multitudo catholicorum omnium, qui fuerunt a tempori-

6. Part 2, the *Compendium errorum Papae*, is relatively modest in length; *Dialogus*,
957–76. Cf. LdM, vol. 9, 178–82 (J. Miethke).

bus prophetarum et apostolorum usque modo, quam evangelio: non quia de evangelio sit aliqualiter dubitandum, sed quia totum maius est sua parte.

Ecclesia ergo, quae maioris auctoritatis est quam evangelista, est illa ecclesia, cuius auctor evangelii pars esse dignoscitur.

2. HERMANN VON SCHILDESCHE (d. 1357)

Hermann von Schildesche (born near Bielefeld in the German province of Westphalia) was a member of the order of the Hermit Friars of St. Augustine, and became one of the scholarly heavyweights of his order. His contemporaries honored him as the *doctor germanus* and *magnus legista*. He wrote his antiheretical treatise in 1330, at the request of Pope John XXII, the pope from whom William of Occam had taken flight a few years previously.[7]

Text

/20–23/ . . . In our view, the beginning of all articles of the faith lies in believing in the holy church. This can be proven by a threefold line of argument, a threefold authority: Christ, the apostles, and Augustine, or the saints. [. . .]

/31–37/ The first reason is derived from the origin of the articles of the faith. . . . Every articulation of our faith derives from the faith with which we believe in the holy church. This is apparent from the fact that the first profession of the faith . . . came about in the early church, the church of the apostles. . .[8]

/47–48, 53–57, 57–59/ The second reason . . . is as follows . . . : If you take away the faith with which we believe in the holy church, we fall prey to doubt about all the other articles of the faith. And this is precisely the view of Augustine in his work *Contra epistolam fundamenti Manichaeorum.* . . . For which reason he speaks to Mani as follows: "If you weakened the authority of the Catholic faith community for me, I would not be able to believe in the gospel, either, because it was precisely through this community of faith that I came to believe the gospel. In this way the gospel would lose all power to convince me, whatever you might adduce from it."[9]

7. RE 7:711–12 (Herman Haupt). Cf. LdM, vol. 4, 2169 (A. Zumkeller) and section 1 above (William of Occam), commentary.

8. From the fourth to the fifteenth or sixteenth century, the consensus of opinion was that the twelve articles of the faith were composed by the apostles, which is why they were known collectively as the Apostles' Creed (*Symbolum Apostolicum*). In fact, the articles in their current form go back to the fifth century, but the individual articles almost all occur in writings from the second century onward; *Theologisch Woordenboek*, Roermond (Maaseik, 1958), 3:4450–54.

9. MSL 42:176. Cf. introduction, n.1.

/62–67/ The third reason derives from the fact that the holy church handed down the books to us, and also sanctioned them. Those books are the source of all the articles of the faith. The third reason, thus, is as follows: That whereby we believe the Scripture is the fundamental principle of the articles of the faith. But this belief in the Scripture comes about because we believe in the church. And this is why Augustine states, in the above-mentioned passage: "I would not believe the gospel if the authority of the holy church did not move me to do so."[10]

/77–83/ This is also the view of the apostle (Rom. 10:14f.), where he states: "For faith stems from hearing, but hearing stems from the word of Christ." The word of Christ is proclaimed by those who preach the gospel, and these preachers are sent by the church. Thus from start to finish this means: (1) Faith comes from hearing; (2) this faith comes to us through the church; and (3) we hold firm to this faith because we believe in the holy church.

/92–96/ This is the view of Augustine in his *Contra epistolam fundamenti*, which he concludes as follows: "It is for this reason that so many strong, most glorious Christian chains rightly bind the believer within the Catholic Church, despite the fact that the sluggishness of our understanding and the impoverishedness with which we shape our lives display the truth in so weak a light."[11]

Commentary

Hermann von Schildesche's interpretation of Augustine's dictum would be difficult to trump when it comes to the support and respect it reveals for the authority of the church. It takes a clear stance, and at first sight there seems to be little that one could object to. Without much ado, Hermann speaks of faith as believing in the church. And it is this church that has the last word, not Scripture.

The reasoning is clear, but nonetheless misleading, or perhaps one should say obfuscatory. Not once does the above passage refer to the pope, and yet effectively the church and the pope are equated with one another. The doctrinal authority of the church is central, and the doctrinal authority of the pope is at the fundamental core. This is stipulated unequivocally in canon law, as expressed in the *Corpus Iuris Canonici*. The renowned bull *Unam sanctam*, issued by Pope Boniface VIII (d. 1302), is merely the finishing touch to a development that had been in progress for centuries.[12]

10. Ibid., n. 4.
11. Ibid., 175.
12. ". . . in der wohl berühmstesten Bulle des Mittelalters, in der Bulle Unam Sanctam (1302) . . ." Horst Fuhrmann, *Einladung ins Mittelalter*, 2nd ed. (Munich, 2002), 130. Cf. chap. 2, n. 143.

The heading that Hermann von Schildesche gives to his treatise is also a very clear statement of his position: "Treatise against the heretics who deny the immunity and jurisdiction of the holy church."[13] This unambiguously refers to the infallible doctrinal authority of the pope.

In this light, William of Occam's interpretation of Augustine's dictum seems all the more remarkable, since William dares to sever precisely this identification between the church and the pope.

Latin Text

From Hermanni de Scildis, OSA, *Tractatus contra haereticos negantes immunitatem et iurisdictionem sanctae ecclesiae* . . . , ed. Adolar Zumkeller (Würzburg, 1970), 5–8.

/20–23/ . . . principium omnium articulorum fidei quoad nos est credere in sanctam Ecclesiam. Quod potest probari triplici ratione et triplici auctoritate, scilicet Christi, Apostoli et Augustini vel sanctorum.

/31–37/ Prima ergo ratio sumitur ex articulorum origine . . . ex fide qua credimus in sanctam Ecclesiam, derivatur ad nos omnis nostrae fidei dearticulatio. Quod patet, quia primum symbolum . . . editum fuit per primitivam ecclesiam apostolorum.

/47–48, 53–57, 57–59/ Secunda ratio . . . est talis . . . : submota fide, qua credimus in sanctam Ecclesiam, circa omnes alios articulos vacillamus. Et haec est sententia Augustini in libro Contra epistolam fundamenti Manichaeorum. . . . Unde dicit sic contra Manichaeum: 'Si infirmabis mihi Catholicorum auctoritatem, iam nec Evangelio credere potero, quia per eos illi credideram. Ita nihil apud me valebit, quidquid inde protuleris.'

/62–67/ Tertia ratio sumitur ex eo, quod sancta Ecclesia tradidit et authenticavit nobis libros, unde omnes articuli colliguntur, et est talis: Illud est nobis principium articulorum fidei, per quod credimus Scripturae, unde articuli colliguntur; sed hoc est ex eo, quod credimus in sanctam Ecclesiam. Unde dicit Augustinus ubi supra: 'Evangelio non crederem, nisi me sanctae Ecclesiae commoveret auctoritas.'

/77–83/ Haec est etiam sententia Apostoli (Ad) Romanos 10, ubi sic arguit: 'Ergo fides ex auditu est, auditus autem per verbum Christi,' verbum Christi per praedicantes, praedicantes vero per Ecclesiam mittentem. Ergo a primo ad ultimum: Fides, quae ex auditu est, derivatur ad nos per Ecclesiam et ex eo, quod in sanctam Ecclesiam credimus, tali fide firmiter inhaeremus.

---

13. The full title of Hermann's work (see above).

/92–96/ Et ista est sententia Augustini Contra epistolam fundamenti, ubi sic concludit: 'Ista ergo tot et tanta nominis christiani clarissima vincula recte hominem tenent credentem in catholica Ecclesia, etiamsi propter nostrae intelligentiae tarditatem vel vitae meritum veritas nondum apertissime se ostendat.'

3. GREGORY OF RIMINI (d. 1358)

Gregory of Rimini was a contemporary of Hermann von Schildesche, and he too was an Augustinian friar.[14] But here the similarities between the two end. Their theological approaches are worlds apart, and their interpretations of Augustine's statement are almost diametrically opposed.

Gregory has an independent and original approach. As a theologian, he is very much his own man, critical and imposing *(doctor authenticus)*. In matters of logic he draws freely on Aristotle, but his theological thinking is colored by Augustine, perhaps more than all the other nominalist theologians.

Gregory's God is a personal, sovereign deity, who is absolutely free and who in his boundless love grants humankind similar freedom. But humankind cannot make claims on God's grace for any petty trivialities. Gregory's anti-Pelagian stance meant that Martin Luther held him in particularly high esteem.[15]

(Gregory of Rimini espoused Augustine's doctrine of double predestination, and also his rigorous teaching on original sin. This led Gregory to the thorny issue of unbaptized children. "Augustine, too, encountered this insoluble problem,"[16] as Gregory says. But though the church father's statements on the matter are extremely dubious, to put it mildly, it was Gregory of Rimini's name that was besmirched. For, sadly, this gifted theologian has gone down in history as the "child-torturer" [*tortor infantium*].[17])

Text

/20:1–4/ The principles of theology, . . . which are acquired through theological discussions, are the truths of the sacred books themselves. For these truths are the point on which the ultimate resolution of the theologians' entire dis-

14. TRE 14:181–84 (Damasus Trapp). See also LdM, vol. 4, 1684–85 (A. Zumkeller).
15. According to Luther, the only scholastics who could be categorized as anti-Pelagian with regard to their views on free will were Gregory of Rimini and Karlstadt; *Resolutiones super propositionibus Lipsiae disputatis* (1519); WA 2:391–435, esp. 394f.
16. *insolubile argumentum quod etiam . . . tangit Augustinus*; TRE 14:182.
17. LThK 4:683.

course is oriented, and from which all theological conclusions are primarily deduced.

[Gregory proceeds to discuss the theological merit of these conclusions in more detail, referring to two writings of Augustine, his *De Trinitate* and his *De doctrina Christiana*.[18] Gregory then formulates the following objection to the principle outlined above.]

/20:21–27/ Against this—that is to say, against what was stated above about the principles of theology—one can argue, as is stated in Aristotle's *Topicorum 1*,[19] that principles "command belief not by virtue of external factors, but of themselves." The authoritative statements contained in the sacred books, however, are not credible of themselves, but draw their credibility from something external to themselves. Think, for example, of the authority of the church, according to that well-known statement by Augustine in his *Contra epistolam fundamenti*, chapter 2: "I would not believe the gospel, did not the authority of the Catholic Church move me to do so."[20] And later: "The Catholics precipitated my belief in the gospel."[21] And he makes many similar statements in the same work.

[Gregory raises three further objections, but he devotes by far the most attention to this first one.]

/21:16–30/ Where the first is concerned, I advance the following objection to the major premise [of the argument]: Principles are not made credible by external factors. That is true. But this should not be taken to mean that there can be no mainspring external to these principles that might lead one to concur with these principles. For this is patently false. What about the principles that are derived from specific experiences? In such cases, it is the experience that leads one to concur with the principles. And these in turn are based on a series of individual observations, as Aristotle states in his *Analytica Posteriora* (near the end)[22] and in the introduction to his *Metaphysica*.[23] What it does mean is this: principles are not credible by virtue of other *principles*, which would be necessary to prove the original ones—as though agreeing with the latter principles constituted grounds for agreeing with the original ones. And in that sense I deny the second part, the minor premise of the argument.

Augustine's authorititative status does not detract from this in any way. For after all, Augustine does not say that he believes the gospel because he finds

18. Augustine, *De Trinitate* 14, 1, 3; MSL 42:1037. Idem, *De doctrina christiana* 2, 42, 63; MSL 34:65.

19. Aristotle, *Topica* 1, 1; 100a30–b19.

20. Augustine, *Contra Epistulam quam vocant fundamenti* 5, 6; MSL 42:176.

21. Ibid.

22. Aristotle, *Analytica posteriora* 2, 19; 100a4–9.

23. Aristotle, *Metaphysica* 1, 1; 980b28–981a17.

agreement with some other principle that demonstrates, or proves by means of a syllogism, that the gospel is true. No, he merely states that for him the authority of the church is a compelling cause to believe the gospel.

This manner of speaking amounts to the same thing as if someone were to say, "I would not believe in the gospel if the sanctity of the church did not move me to do so"; or if, in Christ's own day, a believer had said, "I would not believe /22/ the gospel were it not that the miracles of Christ move me to do so." In these sorts of statements one can indeed discern a certain stimulus to believe the gospel, but not some sort of first principle that would give grounds for believing in the gospel.

Commentary

This passage is taken from Gregory of Rimini's commentary on the first book of the *Sentences* of Peter Lombard (d. 1160). Lombard's *Sentences* constituted a summary of the theology of his day and became the standard theological handbook of the Middle Ages.

Gregory of Rimini's interpretation of Augustine's dictum stands out in the current series; it is a genre unto itself and has little in common with the other viewpoints. There are two reasons for this. First, Gregory explains Augustine's point by drawing on Aristotle's writings on logic—especially his theory of principles (*principia*). Second, Gregory's approach takes the form of a syllogism, a scholastic manner of reasoning in which two propositions—the [*propositio*] *maior* and the [*propositio*] *minor*—are compared with one another. The comparison between the two results in the *conclusio*.

The prologue opens with the fundamental question of what the first principles (*principia*) of theology are. Gregory's answer is measured and apposite: the principles of theology are the truths of the Scriptures themselves. This is the first proposition (*maior*): In Augustine's statement the gospel takes on the significance of a *principle*, which is credible of itself. But it is precisely as his main objection (in addition to a further three) to this rather self-evident proposition that Gregory adduces Augustine's dictum: "I would not believe the gospel if the authority of the Catholic Church did not move me to do so." This is the second proposition (*minor*): for does this not suggest that the authority of the church is the true first principle on which the gospel is ultimately merely dependent?

Gregory responds to this objection with a fascinating and astute analysis of the functioning of principles. His interpretation finally leads to the conclusion that in Augustine's dictum the authority of the church does not take on the role of a principle but of a spur, a stimulus. This is how this theologian seeks to throw light on the problematic relationship between the Scriptures and the church. His style is perhaps not the most elegant, but his reasoning testifies to great power of thought, fully earning him his place in this brief anthology.

Latin Text

From Gregorii Ariminensis, OESA, *Lectura super primum et secundum sententiarum*, ed. A. Damasus Trapp, OESA, Venicio Marcolino, vol. 1, *Super primum. Prologus*, ed. Willigis Eckermann, OESA, collaborante Manfred Schulze (Berlin, New York, 1981), 20–22.

/20:1–4/ Principia theologiae . . . quae scilicet per theologicos discursus acquiritur, sunt ipsae sacri canonis veritates, quoniam ad ipsas stat ultimata resolutio totius discursus theologici et ex eis primo cunctae conclusiones theologicae deducuntur.

/20:21–27/ Sed contra hoc, quod dictum est de principiis theologiae, potest argui, quia, ut dicitur 1 Topicorum, principia sunt 'quae non per alia, sed per se ipsa habent fidem'; sed auctoritates contentae in sacro canone non per se ipsas, sed per alia habent fidem, puta per auctoritatem ecclesiae, iuxta illud Augustini Contra Epistolam fundamenti capitulo 2: "Ego evangelio non crederem, nisi me ecclesiae catholicae commoveret auctoritas," et infra: Catholicis 'praecipientibus evangelio credidi'; et ibidem plura similia dicit.

/21:16–30/ Ad primum dico ad maiorem quod non est intelligendum quod principia non habent fidem per alia, sic quod nihil aliud ab ipsis principiis, sit causa assentiendi eis. Nam hoc est falsum, sicut patet in principiis, quae sumuntur ex experientiis singularium, quorum assensus causa est experimentum, cuius causa etiam fuerunt experientiae multae singularium, ut dicitur 2 Posteriorum in fine et in prooemio Metaphysicae, sed intelligendum est quod non habent fidem per alia, supple, principia, ex quibus ipsa demonstrentur, ita quod assensus illorum sit per se causa assensus circa ipsa. Et ad hunc sensum nego minorem.

Nec auctoritas Augustini est contra, quoniam Augustinus non dicit se credere evangelio propter assensum, quem habeat ad aliquod aliud principium, ex quo evangelium demonstretur vel syllogistice probetur esse verum, sed solum ex auctoritate ecclesiae tamquam ex causa movente ipsum ad fidem evangelii; et est quasi simile huic dicto, quod iste vel alius dicere potuisset: Non crederem evangelio, nisi me ecclesiae sanctitas commoveret, vel si tempore Christi dixisset aliquis credentium: Non crede-/22/rem evangelio, nisi Christi miracula me moverent. Ex quibus dictis, etsi fidei evangelii causa aliqua assignaretur in talibus, non tamen aliquod principium prius, cuius fide causa esset, ut evangelio crederetur.

4. PIERRE D'AILLY (d. 1420)

The texts by Pierre d'Ailly chosen for the current anthology/overview were published as part of the collected works of Jean Gerson (d. 1429). Historically speaking, it is impossible to refer to these two French theologians, Pierre d'Ailly and Jean Gerson, in one breath.[24] Nevertheless, the two do have a lot in common. They both came from northern France, both studied in Paris, and both quickly won acclaim in that city; each was the author of an extensive oeuvre of theological works. Like Pierre d'Ailly, Gerson wrote about mysticism, in his *De mystica theologia*.[25] Both, finally, were chancellor in their turn of the most mighty educational establishment of the Middle Ages, the University of Paris.

Text

/665H–666A/ The term "militant church" can be understood in two ways. The first meaning is that of "the universal church." According to this meaning, there is only one church, and there can be no salvation outside this church. And it is of this that the apostle says (Col. 1:18): *Christ is the head of the body, the church*. And his body is the church. The other meaning is that of "an individual church." In this sense, there are many churches. And this is what is referred to in another statement by the same apostle: *All the churches of Christ greet you* (Rom. 16:16).

/666A/ In each of the two senses mentioned, the term can be understood in many different ways. If I speak of the universal church, this sometimes has the meaning of the congregation of all believers who are now alive. Sometimes the meaning is more general, and may refer to the congregation of all the faithful who have succeeded one another from the time of Christ and the apostles until the present day. This is how the term is used to distinguish the church of Christ from the synagogue of Moses. And it is in this sense that Augustine understands the term "church" in his book *Contra Manichaeos*, as quoted in canon *Palam* in *Distinctio XI* and elsewhere.[26] There he says that he would not believe the gospel were it not that the authority of the church

24. For Pierre d'Ailly, see TRE 26:278–81 (Francis Oakley); for Jean Gerson, see TRE 12:532–38 (Christoph Burger). Lit. ibid. 536–38. For Gerson's interpretation of Augustine's dictum, see G. H. M. Posthumus Meyjes, *Jean Gerson. Apostle of Unity: His Church Politics and Ecclesiology*, trans. J. C. Grayson (Leiden, Boston: Brill, 1999), 172, 216–17, 321–22.

25. Ioannis Carlerii de Gerson, *De mystica theologia*, ed. André Combes (Lugano [1958]).

26. See above (William of Occam), n. 1. Pierre is referring here to Augustine's *Liber contra epistulam Fundamenti*.

compelled him to do so. In this sense the authority of the church is greater than that of the gospel, because the evangelist, or the author of the gospel, is part of this church.

/691A/ [In his reflections on the universal church, d'Ailly also addresses the topic of] . . . the office instituted by Christ. This includes the pope and all others who are rightfully at his side. If a chair falls vacant, the church in this sense continues to exist only in those in whom the authority of this council is invested. . . . Taking this as given, the train of thought[27] runs as follows: The Church of Rome understood in this way is part of the universal church; nevertheless it cannot deviate from the rules ordained by the law of Christ. For if the Church of Rome were to deviate significantly from these rules, it follows that the universal church would also deviate. And this is proved as follows: Christ ordained that the universal church should not be able to deviate from his law, and for this reason he ordained that the individual church [the Church of Rome], which has the power to judge authoritatively on behalf of the universal church, should not be able to err. For the Lord constituted this church the head of the universal church. This is clear from the initial premise above, and is confirmed in the decretals, *Distinctio XXII Sacrosancta*: "If the head is lacking in sense, the limbs also go astray."[28]

[Pierre d'Ailly then /691B/ adduces the testimony of various church fathers—Ambrose, Jerome, and Cyprian—and points to the structures of authority in the Old Testament (Deut. 17). Finally, after the three other church fathers, he alludes to Augustine's statement.]

/691B/ The fourth argument is taken from Augustine, in his work *Contra Epistolam Fundamenti Manichaei, cap. II*, where he says: "I would not believe the gospel were it not that the authority of the Catholic Church moves me to do so." But this authority resides principally in the church that is the head of the other churches, as explained above. Ergo . . .

/691C–D/ . . . The answer to this is that even the individual Church of Rome is not the head of the universal church, nor does the aforementioned authority reside in it, except on the condition that the Church of Rome itself remains steadfast in the true Faith. Certainly the Church of Rome did itself receive this true faith from the blessed Peter, but this does not mean that it

27. I.e., of those who identify the "church" with the Church of Rome.

28. Canon *Sacrosancta* stresses the primacy of the *Romana et Apostolica Ecclesia*. This primacy was bestowed on the Roman Catholic Church "not by the apostles, but by the Lord himself, our Redeemer." It is not clear whether Pierre d'Ailly is quoting an existing saying or proverb, or simply drawing a conclusion from canon *Sacrosancta*. The expression is strongly reminiscent of Rom. 12:4–8; 1 Cor. 12:12–26; and also Eph. 1:22. The image of the body and its limbs also occurs relatively frequently in Greek and Roman literature; cf. *Internationaal Commentaar op de Bijbel*, 2 vols. (Kok-Kampen, Averbode, 2001), 2:1883.

could not lose it! Remember the church of Antioch![29] Remember also the consequences of this. If the church of Antioch itself had become unbelieving or heretical, those who were formerly the Church of Rome would have ceased to be the head of the church. They would have lost their leading position and their aforementioned authority. But even then the faith of the universal church would not have been lost.

And my response to that saying about common sense being lacking in the limbs if it is lacking in the head is as follows: there are indeed many ways in which one can liken the mystical body of Christ, the church, to the material body of a human being. But the comparison does not hold on all fronts. /692A/ For the body of a human being cannot remain alive without a head, whereas the body of the church does remain alive—in the sense of the life of faith and grace—in the absence of a head on earth, for example, if there is no pope. For the church still has its heavenly head, Christ. He is the head of the church, as it says in Eph. 1:22. And even if the Church of Rome—not counting the pope[a]—is the most important limb of the church and could for this reason be called its head, nevertheless the church could continue to exist without it. Ergo . . .

/692B/ And as far as Augustine's authority is concerned, he is speaking—as was said above—not about the individual Church of Rome, but about the universal church. This is evident, first of all, because it would be absurd to say that we should accord the authority of any individual church more credibility than the gospel. Secondly, it is clear from Augustine's words. For after all, he speaks of the church which has been in existence from the days of Peter to his own time, which means that it includes Peter and the other apostles and evangelists and all the saints who have received the gospel and propagated the teachings of Christ. And in this sense the authority of that church is greater than that of the gospel. Etc.

Commentary

Pierre d'Ailly chooses to understand the term "church" in Augustine's statement in the broadest possible sense of the word. In content, and sometimes even in wording, his interpretation bears a strong resemblance to that of William of Occam. But had the controversy between the canon lawyers and the theologians that the Englishman had observed many years before been set aside in the meantime? Not in the slightest! No, the situation of the church

29. The above-mentioned canon *Sacrosancta* also reports that *"before he came to Rome,"* Peter lived in Antioch (in Syria). Cf. Gal. 2:11–14.
a. An extremely concise turn of phrase! Given the context, this translation seems to make the most sense.

had gone dramatically downhill, and the schism in the Western church had divided the faithful since 1378. Two, and later three, rival popes would rend Western Christendom apart.

Both Jean Gerson and Pierre d'Ailly felt the catastrophe of the Great Schism very keenly. Gerson writes emotionally of the matter in his *Trilogus in materia schismatis* (1402–03),[30] where he laments: "*Is it not desperately, deeply sad, a sorrow without all parallel: this schism is a plague on us, a sorrow greater than any ever witnessed hitherto.*"[31] But the two Frenchmen also contributed significantly to the efforts to restore the unity of the Western church. They were among the architects of the conciliar theory which smoothed the way for the eventual election of a new pope (Martin V) at the Council of Constance (1414–18).

In the above text by Pierre d'Ailly, one can discern the clear outlines of the foundations of this theological theory, i.e., that the general council is the supreme authority in the church, higher even than the pope. However, Pierre d'Ailly's approach is underpinned by his invoking the authority of the Scriptures, and he does this on two separate occasions in the above passage.

It seems to me that theology has won the day this time.

Latin Text

From P. de Alliaco, *Utrum Petri Ecclesia Lege gubernetur*, in Jean Gerson, *Opera omnia*, ed. L. E. Dupin (Antwerp, 1706), I, 665–66, 691–92.

/665H–666A/ Ecclesia Militans dupliciter potest sumi. Uno modo pro Ecclesia universali, et sic est unica Ecclesia et extra quam non est salus, de qua dicit Apostolus: *Coloss.* 1:18, quod Christus *est caput corporis Ecclesiae*, et corpus ejus est Ecclesia. Alio modo pro Ecclesia particulari: et sic sunt plures Ecclesiae juxta illud dictum ejusdem Apostoli: *Salutant vos omnes Ecclesiae Christi*, Rom. xvi.16.

/666A/ Utroque autem praedictorum modorum adhuc multipliciter sumitur Ecclesia. Nam sumendo eam pro Ecclesia universali quandoque sumitur pro congregatione omnium fidelium actu existentium. Quandoque vero generalius sumitur pro congregatione omnium fidelium a tempore Christi vel Apostolorum usque nunc succedentium; et sic distinguitur Ecclesia Christi contra Synagogam Moysi. Et isto modo accipit Augustinus Ecclesiam in Libro *Contra Manichaeos*, ut habetur XI *Distinctio caput Palam* et alibi. Ubi dicit quod Evangelio non crederet, nisi eum Ecclesiae autoritas compelleret.

---

30. See *Trilogus in materia schismatis. Oeuvres Complètes.* Introduction, texte et notes by monseigneur Glorieux (Paris, etc., 1960–68), vol. 6, *L'oeuvre ecclesiologique*, no. 264, 69–96.
31. Op. cit., 72.

Hoc enim modo Ecclesia est majoris autoritatis quam Evangelium sit; quia hujus Ecclesiae Evangelista seu scriptor Evangelii pars existit.

/691A/ . . . Ecclesiae, secundum ordinem a Christo institutum; quae scilicet complectitur Papam et alios rite ad suum Collegium pertinentes, et vacante Sede salvatur in illis solis, in quibus est autoritas Concilii sui . . .

Hoc supposito arguit sic: Romana Ecclesia sic sumpta est pars universalis Ecclesiae; et tamen non potest difformari regulae Legis Christi: quia ad eam sic difformari sequitur Ecclesiam universalem illi regulae difformari, quod probat: quia sicut Christus ordinavit quod Ecclesia universalis non possit difformari suae Legi, ita etiam ordinavit quod illa Ecclesia particularis, penes quam residet autoritative Judicium universalis Ecclesiae, non possit errare, cum ipsa sit a Domino constituta tanquam caput universalis Ecclesiae, ut patet ex suppositione et etiam in Decretis, XXII *Distinctio Sacrosancta*. Sed deficientibus sensibus in capite deficient [sensus] in membris.

/691B/ . . . Quarta est Augustini in Libello contra Epistolam Fundamenti Manichaei, *caput II* dicentis: *Ego Evangelio non crederem, nisi me Ecclesiae Catholicae commoveret autoritas:* sed haec autoritas principaliter residet in illa Ecclesia quae est caput aliarum, modo praedicto. Quare etc.

/691C-D/ . . . Respondetur quod ipsa particularis Ecclesia Romana non est caput universalis Ecclesiae nec apud eam residet autoritas praedicta, nisi sub conditione, scilicet quamdiu ipsa manet in Fide recta. Nam licet ipsa in Beato Petro recepit eam, tamen nihil videtur prohibere quin eam possit perdere sicut in Ecclesia Antiochena et ita tamen, si ipsa fieret infidelis aut haeretica, illi qui prius erant Ecclesia Romana desinerent esse caput Ecclesiae nec haberent talem principatum aut autoritatem praedictam; nec propter hoc deficeret Fides Ecclesiae universalis.

Et quando dicitur quod deficientibus sensibus in capite deficiunt in membris etc., respondi quod, licet quantum ad multa sit similitudo inter corpus Christi mysticum, quod est Ecclesia, et corpus materiale hominis, tamen non in omnibus est similitudo, quia /692A/ corpus hominis non manet vivus sine capite, corpus autem Ecclesiae manet vivum, scilicet vita Fidei et gratiae absque capite in terris, ut puta dum caret Summo Pontifice. Tamen tunc habet caput in coelis, scilicet Christum, qui est caput Ecclesiae ut dicitur *Ephes.* 1:22. Et quamvis Romana Ecclesia post Papam sit ipsius Ecclesiae membrum principale et ratione ipsius possit dici caput ejus, tamen sine ipsa posset esse Ecclesia. Quare etc.

/692B/ Ad autoritatem Augustini dictum est, quod non loquitur de particulari Ecclesia Romana, sed de Ecclesia universali. Quod patet primo, quia absurdum esset dicere quod autoritati alicujus particularis Ecclesiae esset magis credendum quam Evangelio. Secundo patet ex verbis Augustini, quia loquitur ibi de Ecclesia quae successit a tempore Petri usque ad tempus suum et sic ipsa comprehendit Petrum et alios Apostolos ac Evangelistas et Sanctos omnes, a quibus in Ecclesia susceptum est Evangelium et publicata doctrina Christi. Et sic major est illius Ecclesiae autoritas quam Evangelii etc.

5. THOMAS NETTER WALDENSIS (d. 1430)

Thomas Netter Waldensis, from Saffron Walden in Essex, who studied in Oxford, also experienced the shattering of the Western church by the Great Schism. He took part in two great councils of his day: the Council of Pisa (1409) and the Council of Constance (1414–18). He attended the latter in his capacity as provincial of the Carmelite Order.

Text

/348C–D/ The authority of the universal church is subordinate to the authority of the Scriptures of both the Old and the New Testament.

SYNOPSIS OF THIS CHAPTER
1. What some have been so bold as to assert regarding Augustine's dictum: "*I would not believe the gospel if the authority of the Catholic Church did not move me to do so.*"
2. *The authority of the Scripture exceeds the authority of all the doctors [of the church] and of the Catholic Church as a whole.*
3. *Witnesses are one thing, the actual testimony itself quite another. The testimony of the Catholic Church is the object of Christian faith.*
4. *This definition of the universal church is very close to the truth: one faith, on which all the holy doctors [of the church] agree.*

1. The universal church's achievements in the past must be sufficient for it to propagate its power in modern times. The glory of its power should take wing from that past to the latter generations, as though flying over the empire of some majestic ruler: in such a way that even now /349A–C/ it should not be possible to read any Scripture, or regard it as certain, without the authority of that universal church. This is what Augustine meant when he said in his *Contra Epistolam fundamenti*—just after the beginning, in chapter 5: "*I would not believe the gospel, were it not that the authority of the Catholic Church moves me to do so.*" Thus speaks Augustine.[32]

Nevertheless, I do not approve of the supercilious tone that some people adopt at this point. They take this statement as a cue to claim that the things decreed by the fathers and the church bear greater authority, validity, and

---

32. See introduction, n. 1.

weight than the authority of the Scriptures. This is not only inaccurate, but foolish. For these people would then have to say that Philip was greater than Christ, when he brought Nathanael to believe that Christ was indeed the one of whom Moses had written in the Law and the Prophets (John 1:45). But without Christ's authority, he [Nathanael] would have noticed nothing. If that were the case, one would have to say, equally, that our natural parents or tutors were higher and more important than Christ, since it is through their influence that we have learned, from our earliest infancy, what we should believe—and what we may hope—of Christ.

But see what Augustine says in his *De Magistro*, slightly more than half-way, in book I, chapter 8, at the beginning: "Something that is there, he says, because of something else, is necessarily inferior to that to which owes its existence. You know the name of a by-product. The name from which the byproduct takes its name must be ranked more highly than the name of the byproduct itself." Thus writes Augustine.[33]

2. Thus since the purpose of all ecclesiastical authority is to bear witness to Christ and his laws, it must be inferior to the laws of Christ. It is thus necessarily subordinate to the sacred Scriptures. And Augustine says the same thing in book 12 of his *Contra Faustum*, chapter 96, where he speaks of the holy books, saying. . . .[34]

/349D/ This is the way it is: the canonical Scriptures have divine authority. All humankind, with all its reason, is subject to these Scriptures. St. Thomas drew up an interesting allegory in this matter,[35] with the Samaritan woman representing the universal church. When the people heard her talking of Christ and saying: "He told me everything I had ever done," they also became believers, and said: "It is no longer because of what you said that we believe, for we have heard for ourselves, and we know that this is truly the Savior of the world" (John 4:42). It is not that they are ungrateful because, in bowing to the authority of him in whom they believe, they no longer believe on the basis of what the woman said. Rather, they were brought to the faith by the authority of that woman. For the text goes: "many believed in him because of the words of the woman who gave testimony of him."[36] That is the origin of their faith. In the same way, the children of mother church are also not ungrateful in believing in the first instance because of the words of the church that testifies of Christ. Once they believe, they rank the authority through which they came to believe below the authority of him in whom they believe. Indeed, by the authority of that same church it has been decreed that the books of all

33. Augustine, *De magistro* 1, 8; MSL 32:1209–10.
34. Augustine, *Contra Faustum* 22, 96; CSEL 25:702–3.
35. Thomas Aquinas, *Summa theologiae* 2.2.q.2, a.10.
36. John 4:39.

people *and* of their churches from later times must submit to the authority of the sacred canon like /350A/ "a footstool under their feet."[37] Thus writes Augustine in book 11 of his *Contra Faustum, caput V* . . .[38]

/350C/ The authority of the Holy Scriptures is thus by far the greatest. It exceeds the authority of all the *doctores*, even of the entire Catholic Church. Notwithstanding this, however, the Catholic Church must attest the authority of the Scriptures.

Commentary

For Thomas Netter, too, the concept of the universal church is central, and he speaks of it in lavish and even rather triumphalist terms: "the glory of its power" and "the empire of a majestic ruler." Augustine's dictum about the authority of the church would seem to lend itself perfectly for underpinning this vision. But Thomas does not yield to this temptation; his interpretation of the church father's words is finely nuanced and critical. Thomas believes that the dictum has been misunderstood. In crystal clear terms, he places the authority of the Scriptures above that of the church.

At the same time, he makes a strong case for the essential function fulfilled by the church. The subtle distinction that he draws between witnesses and testimony is enlightening. Another interesting feature here is his comparison with the testimony of the Samaritan woman from John 4, an allegory he attributes to Thomas Aquinas.

Thomas Netter's conviction that the church fulfills a vital function explains why this theologian was an outspoken opponent of John Wycliffe and John Hus. In holding that it is only the written word, the Holy Scripture, that counts, Wycliffe cuts Christian faith in two, Thomas contends.[39] He regards this approach as shortsighted, since *"custom itself is the living faith of the Church."*[40]

Thomas Netter does not argue in scholastic terms, but rather along biblical or patristic lines. Nevertheless, his meaning is not always entirely clear. The *Doctrinale*, his main work, was extremely influential; it was printed three times in the sixteenth century, and even attained one imprint in the eighteenth century.[41]

37. Ps. 110:1.
38. Augustine, *Contra Faustum* 11, 5; CSEL 25:320–21.
39. RE 13:749–53 (R. Seeberg), here p. 750, 14–15. See also LdM, 8:725–26 (K. Walsh).
40. *Ipsa consuetudo est animata fides ecclesiae;* RE 13:750, 41–42.
41. Op. cit., 753, 41–42. It is unfortunately beyond the scope of the present study to determine which edition of Augustine's work Netter consulted for his *Doctrinale*.

Latin Text

From Thomas Waldensis carmelitae anglici, *Doctrinale antiquitatum fidei catholicae ecclesiae*, ed. F. Bonaventura Blanciotti, Tomus primus (Venice, 1757), 348D–350C.

/348C–D/ Quod authoritas universalis Ecclesiae subdita est authoritati Scripturarum tam novi quam veteris testamenti.

SYNOPSIS CAPITIS

1. *Quid occasione Augustinianae illius sententiae,* Evangelio non crederem, nisi me Ecclesiae Catholicae commoveret authoritas, *quidem asserere ausi fuerint.*
2. *Scripturae authoritas, authoritati cunctorum Doctorum, ac etiam totius Ecclesiae Catholicae supereminet.*
3. *Aliud sunt testes, aliud testimonium; et quod Catholicae ecclesiae testimonium objectum est Christianae fidei.*
4. *Verisimile est esse definitionem universalis Ecclesiae illud, in quo Sancti Doctores una fide conveniunt.*

1. Sufficiat ergo universali Ecclesiae pro praeconio potestatis suae modernae, quod olim hoc fecerit: Unde gloria potestatis ejus, quasi per cujusdam majestatis imperium, volaret ad posteros: ita quod adhuc sine ejus au./349A–C/ thoritate, Scriptura aliqua nec legi poterit nec haberi pro certa[b] Et hoc sapuit, cum diceret *contra Epistolam fundamenti* cito post principium, idest cap. V Augustinus. 'Evangelio non crederem, nisi me Catholicae Ecclesiae commoveret authoritas.' Haec ille.[c]

Nec tamen hic laudo supercilium, quod quidam attollunt volentes occasione hujus dicti decretum Patrum in Ecclesia majoris esse authoritatis, culminis et ponderis quam sit authoritas Scripturarum.[d] Quod quidem non tam videtur ineptum quam fatuum; nisi talis quis dicat Philippum fuisse majorem Christo, quando induxit Nathanaelem ad credendum Christum esse illum quem scripsit Moyses in lege et Prophetis, *Joan.*1,[e] sine cujus[f] authoritate non tunc adverteret. Et si sic, dicat conformiter parentes nostros carnales aut paedagogos esse altiores et eminentiores Christo, quia eorum authoritate ab infantia didicimus quid de Christo sit credendum, quid sperandum. Sed Augustinus in libro suo *de Magistro* post medium, lib. I, cap. VIII in principio. Augustinus:[g] 'Quidquid, inquit, propter aliud est, vilius sit necesse est quam

b. *Adhuc sine Ecclesiae authoritate nec legi nec credi potest Scriptura aliqua* (marg.)
c. *Augustinus To. 8., pag. 154* (marg.)
d. *Supra authoritatem Ecclesiae est authoritas Scripturae Canonicae* (marg.)
e. *Joan. 1.45* (marg.)
f. referring to Christ
g. *Augustinus To. 1, cap. 9, pag. 555* (marg.)

id propter quod est. Cognitio quippe coeni, propter quam hoc nomen est institutum, pluris habenda est ipso nomine.' Haec ille.

2. Omnis ergo Ecclesiastica authoritas cum sit ad testificandum de Christo et legibus ejus, vilior est Christi legibus et Scripturis Sanctis necessario postponenda. Ideo idem Augustinus lib. XXII *Contra Faustum*, caput XCVI de divinis libris loquens . . .[h]

/349D/ Ecce quod Scripturae canonicae habent authoritatem divinam et eis subjiciuntur omnia genera hominum simul et ingeniorum. Bene enim allegorizavit Sanctus Thomas[i] de hac re inducens mulierem Samaritanam loco universalis Ecclesiae; quam cum audissent Cives praedicantem de Christo et dicentem quod *dixit mihi quaecumque feci.*[j] Illi tandem inducti, *jam* (inquiunt) *non propter loquelam tuam credimus: ipsi enim audivimus et scimus quia hic est Salvator mundi,* Joan. 4. Non sunt ingrati, quod non propter loquelam mulieris credunt jam, cum authoritati ejus adhaerent, cui credunt, quamvis ad credendum illi authoritate mulieris inducti sunt. Sic enim dicit textus,[k] quod *multi crediderunt in eum propter verbum mulieris testimonium perhibentis*, principaliter et primo credunt. Sic nec sunt ingrati filii Matris Ecclesiae, qui primo propter verbum Ecclesiae testantis de Christo credunt, et cum crediderint, authoritatem qua inducti sunt authoritati ejus postponunt, cui credunt; immo authoritate ejusdem Ecclesiae hoc decretum est omnium scilicet posteriorum hominum libros sive Ecclesiarum authoritati Sacri canonis debere submitti, quasi /350A/ad scabellum pedum ejus, dicente XI lib. *Contra Faustum, caput V Augustino* . . .[l]

/350C/ Longe ergo distat authoritas Scripturarum et eminet authoritati cunctorum Doctorum, etiam totius Ecclesiae catholicae; quamvis super earum authoritate Catholica attestetur Ecclesia.

6. GABRIEL BIEL (d. 1495)

Gabriel Biel[42] was a highly talented, multifaceted figure, a successful organizer as well as an important churchman (one of the founders of the University of Tübingen). However, in these two texts in which he interprets Augustine's dictum he does not exactly shine with an original theological stance. His own

---

h. *Augustinus To. 8, pag. 420* (marg.)
i. *S. Thomas secunda secundae quaest. 2. artic. 10.* (marg.)
j. *Joan. 4.39. etc.* (marg.)
k. *Joan. 4.39* (marg.)
l. *Augustinus To. 8, pag. 221* (marg.)
42. Cf. H. A. Oberman, op. cit. (n. 56), 9–29. TRE 6:488–91 (Werner Dettloff). *Oeuvre*, 489–510, bibliography, 491. Cf. also LdM, 2:127 (M. Schulze).

religious life was nourished by the spirituality of the *Devotio moderna*. He was in charge of the spiritual guidance of various houses of the Brethren of the Common Life, and perhaps the title "Brother Gabriel" is the most characteristic for him. In that capacity he maintained close contacts with Wessel Gansfort for some time.[43] Just how great the differences between the two were, however, will be immediately apparent from the next of the interpretative passages (see next chapter).

Text I (On the Sentences)

/415, 1–16/ [Thesis: "Acquired faith" is necessary to believe in the articles of the faith.]

1. This conclusion is proven by the authority of the apostle in Romans 10 [verses 17 and 14]: "faith comes from hearing, and hearing comes through the word of God." And before this he says: "And how are they to believe in one of whom they have never heard? And how are they to hear without a preacher?" This cannot be understood to refer to faith that is infused into the believer, because this does not arise from hearing someone preach, but is created directly by God.

2. The thesis is also proven by the argument that Scotus uses here.[44] In order to believe the articles it is necessary to believe in the church, which means believing that the church is truthful; we believe this due to our acquired faith. Thus the thesis is proved. But note the following:

3. The major premise[45] derives from Augustine, in his *Epistula Fundamenti contra Manichaeos*: "I would not believe the gospel," if I did not believe the church.[46] According to Augustine, we cannot believe in the books of the canon and the Scriptures unless we first believe in the church that approves these books and their contents. And even if some books derive their authority from their authors, nevertheless it is possible to advocate them wholeheartedly only if we believe the church, which testifies that the authors of these books are credible.

And that is why Augustine says in the same place: "I do not accept the gospel of the Nazarenes because it is not accepted by the church."[47]

43. M. van Rhijn, *Studiën over Wessel Gansfort en zijn tijd* (Utrecht, 1933), 23.

44. In the Latin text, the passages borrowed from Scotus are marked (> - <), in accordance with the above-mentioned edition of the text.

45. See the commentary on Gregory of Rimini's interpretation above. By contrast—and characteristically—Gabriel Biel refers to Augustine's statement as the *maior [propositio]*.

46. In part, this is the familiar quotation from Augustine's *Contra epistulam fundamenti*. Cf. introduction, n. 1.

47. This saying is nowhere to be found in Augustine's works.

Text II (Canon of the Mass)

[Biel sketches a picture of the church militant and the church victorious. "Nobody outside of this church can be saved, even if he were to spill his own blood in Christ's name."[48]]

/199/ In this sense [i.e., of the church militant] "church" means, on the one hand, the congregation of all the faithful now alive, and this is the true church. In the other sense, it refers to the representative body of the church, which means the general council, gathered together legitimately in the Holy Spirit.

In the interpretation of many, this refers to the church, to which Christ's saying about admonishing one's fellow believer applies: "If he does not listen to you, tell it to the church."[49]

For the true church, the community of all the faithful, is so extensive that it is never congregated together to make a decision; indeed it cannot be gathered together. But fathers are convoked from all parts of the world to assess matters and take decisions. And in doing so, they represent the true church.

In this sense, the church is the highest court on earth, which has authority over each and every individual, no matter how high his eminence or dignity, be he the pope himself.[50] This was laid down very firmly at the Council of Constance, in the decree *Frequens*.[51]

In yet another sense, the church can be taken to mean not only the congregation of all the faithful who are now alive, but also of all those who have ever lived from the time of Christ and the apostles right up until our own day. It is distinct from the synagogue of Moses. This is the sense in which Augustine speaks of the church in his *Epistola Fundamenti*, where he says: *"I would not believe the gospel, were it not that the authority of the church compels me to do so."*[52] And in this sense the church has more authority than the gospel, since the evangelist, the author of the gospel, is part of the church; and the whole has more authority than one part.

And this is also how Augustine understood the term "church" in his *Contra Manichaeos*, quoted in canon *Palam* of *Distinctio XI*,[53] where it says:

> It is clear that in matters of doubt where faith—and certainty about faith—are concerned, the authority of the Catholic Church must have the last word. This is confirmed from the deep-seated authority of the

48. Pseudo-Augustine, *De fide ad Petrum* 2, 39; MSL 40:776.
49. Cf. Matt. 18:17.
50. In part, Biel here follows the wording of the fifth session of the Council of Constance; *Mansi* 27:590. Cf. also Gerson, *Oeuvres Complètes*, no. 282, p. 217.
51. The decree *Frequens* was issued at the thirty-ninth session of the Council of Constance on Oct. 9, 1417; *Mansi* 27:1159; RE 11:30–34 (G. Voigt, B. Bess).
52. See introduction, n. 1.
53. See above, William of Occam, section 1, n. 1.

apostles right up to the present day, in the concurrence of those who
succeed them: the bishops and so many people.[54]

Here "Catholic Church" comprises both the bishops and the people who have
succeeded one another from the days of the apostles right up to the present
day. This is referred to as the Christian church, and has its origin in Christ;
first of all it was in Judea, and at that point it was called the church of Jerusalem—see Acts 8:1: "That day a severe persecution began against the church in
Jerusalem." Second in line was the church of Antioch, where the apostle Peter
first settled and where the word "Christian" was first noted. For this reason,
the faithful were initially called disciples and brothers; afterwards they were
known as Christians.

Commentary

In both of Biel's texts, Augustine's dictum is firmly embedded in the context
of the church. In the first passage this comes to the fore in the heading "Articles of the Faith."[55] Drawing up rules to govern faith is typically the activity
of a church. Biel here draws on the scholastic distinction between "acquired"
and "infused" faith.[56] The former term smacks rather of justification, which
is why Martin Luther, who was full of praise for Biel's *Canonis misse Expositio*,
was rather less enthusiastic about the distinctions he applied to faith.[57]

Biel's primary concern was apparently to stress the authority of the church.
He quotes the second phrase of Augustine's statement in a slightly corrupt
version (". . . if I did not believe in the *church*"). From start to finish—as
the editors of this first passage make clear—Biel's line of argument is heavily
indebted to Duns Scotus (d. 1308).[58] The latter was also his source for the
statement about the gospel of the Nazarenes that he attributes to Augustine.

54. Cf. Occam's version (p. 2 above). Neither reproduces the text of canon *Palam*
entirely verbatim; Occam is slightly freer in his approach. Cf. p. 26, notes n and o.
55. The articles of the faith play an important role in Hermann von Schildesche's
interpretation of Augustine's dictum. See section 2, pp. 5–8.
56. See H. A. Oberman, *The Harvest of Medieval Theology: Gabriel Biel and Late
Medieval Nominalism* (Cambridge, 1963), 68–89 (II Faith: Acquired and Infused).
57. Luther viewed Biel's *Canonis misse Expositio* as "das beste Buch über diesen
Gegenstand" (the best book about this subject); M. Brecht, *Martin Luther. Sein Weg
zur Reformation. 1483–1521*, 2nd ed. (Stuttgart, 1983), 78. "In diesen zentralen Stücken
der Rechtfertigungs- und Gnadenlehre denke er [Biel] pelagianisch"; op. cit., 165. On
the whole, however, Luther's criticism of Biel far outweighs his brief word of praise.
Cf. Tischreden, WA no. 3146 (May 30, 1532) and no. 3722 (Feb. 1538). I am very
grateful to Dr. Frans Pieter van Stam (Amsterdam) for these critical nuances and his
many well-informed suggestions.
58. See the markings in the Latin text (> - <). For Scotus, see chapter 3, n. 113.

The second text is about ecclesiastical gatherings; and there can scarcely be any activity more fundamental to what it means to be a church than that of "gathering together." But this text is imbued with a completely different spirit from the first. Here it is the term "universal church" that forms Biel's starting point. He himself unambiguously professes his allegiance to the Council of Constance.

This second text also leans heavily on the authority of another big name: in this case, William of Occam, who introduced a new direction in theological thinking: nominalism. But Gabriel Biel never actually mentions the big name. Is this deliberate? The extent of Biel's dependence on William's *Dialogus* is quite astonishing![59] Biel must have had the earlier work open on his desk as he wrote. He quotes it verbatim, which helped me in reconstructing the correct text of the *Expositio*.

Latin Text I

From Gabrielis Biel, *Collectorium circa quattuor libros Sententiarum. Liber tertius*, ed. Wilfridus Werbeck and Udo Hofmann (Tübingen, 1979), 415.

(*Collectorium*) 415, 1–16 . . . Fides acquisita ad credendum fidei articulos est necessaria. Probatur illa conclusio auctoritate *Apostoli* Rom. 10 [:17.14]: 'Fides ex auditu est. Auditus autem per verbum Dei.' Et praemisit: >Quomodo credent ei, quem non audierunt, quomodo audient sine praedicante?< Quae non possunt intelligi de fide infusa, quae non est ex auditu praedicationis, sed immediate creata a Deo.

Et probatur ratione *Scoti* distinctione praesenti: Ad credendum articulos necesse est credere ecclesiae, hoc est credere ecclesiam esse veracem; hoc credimus fide acquisita; ergo.

Consequentia nota.

Maior est Augustini in epistola Fundamenti contra Manichaeos: >Evangelio non crederem, nisi< crederem ecclesiae. Ergo secundum eum libris canonis et Scripturae >non est credendum, nisi quia primo credendum est ecclesiae approbanti libros illos et contenta in eis<. Et licet quidam libri auctoritatem >habeant ex auctoribus suis<, tamen firmiter non adhaeretur eis, >nisi quia creditur ecclesiae testificanti veraces esse illorum auctores<. Unde ibidem ait *Augustinus*: >Evangelium Nazaraeorum non admittam. Quia non admittitur ab ecclesia<.

---

59. Biel takes over verbatim Occam's line of argument about the whole (*totum*) being greater than the part (*pars*).

Latin Text II[m]

From Gabrielis Biel, *Canonis misse Expositio*, ed. Heiko A. Oberman and William J. Courtenay, Pars Prima (Wiesbaden, 1963), 199.

(*Canonis misse Expositio m*) /199/ . . . Hoc modo uno modo pro congregatione omnium fidelium actu existentium que est ecclesia vera. Alio modo pro ecclesia representativa, que est concilium generale in spiritu sancto legittime congregatum. De qua ecclesia secundum plurium expositiones intelligitur illud verbum christi de correptione fratris, *si te non audierit dic ecclesiae*, MATTH. xviii[17].

Ecclesia enim vera omnium fidelium multitudo propter suam dilatationem nunquam congregatur, neque congregari potest ad quodcunque discernendum, sed convocantur patres de omnibus mundi partibus qui diffiniunt et decernunt, et hec facientes ecclesiam veram representant. Et sic ecclesia est supremum tribunal in terris habens auctoritatem super quamlibet personam singularem cuiuscunque status eminentie aut dignitatis extiterit, etiam si papalis, prout in constitutione frequens concilii constantiensis clarius diffinitur.

Accipitur etiam adhuc ecclesia pro congregatione, non tantum omnium fidelium existentium, sed omnium qui fuerunt a tempore christi et apostolorum usque nunc sibi succedentium. Et distinguitur a synagoga moysi, et sic accipit Augustinus in EPISTOLA FUNDAMENTI dicens: *Evangelio non crederem nisi ecclesie auctoritas me compelleret.* Hoc enim modo ecclesia maioris ets auctoritatis quam evangelium, quia huius ecclesie evangelista scriptor evangelii est pars, totum autem maioris auctoritatis est sua parte. Hoc modo accepit etiam ecclesiam Augustinus in libro CONTRA MANICHAEOS, et recitatur dist. xi, can. *Palam*, ubi ait: *Palam est quod in re dubia ad fidem* *et certitudinem*[n] *valeat auctoritas ecclesie catholice, que ab ipsis fundatissimis apostolorum sedibus, usque ad hodiernum diem succedentium sibimet, et episcoporum*[o] *et tot populorum consensione firmatur*, ubi ecclesia catholica episcopos et populos a tempore apostolorum usque ad hodiernum diem sibimet succedentes importat. Et hec vocatur ecclesia christiana que cepit ortum a christo, primo in iudea, et vocabatur primo ecclesia hierosolymitana; unde ACT. viii[1]: *Et factum est in illa die persecutio magna in ecclesia que erat in hierosolimis.* Secunda fuit antiochena, in qua apostolus Petrus primum resedit, et ibi primum innotuit nomen 'christianus.' Unde fideles primo vocabantur discipuli et fratres, postea vocati sunt christiani.

m. The text of the *Canonis misse Expositio* is somewhat corrupt in the edition that was available to me. One line is printed twice, and another is entirely lacking. I was able to supply the latter from William of Occam's *Dialogus*, which Biel here quotes verbatim. This dependence on William of Occam was overlooked by the editors.

n. *--* Addition by William of Occam, adopted by Biel.

o. The word *serie* is lacking in Biel's quotation.

2

Who Has Authority in the Church?

1. WESSEL GANSFORT'S INTERPRETATION

Introduction

This chapter provides yet another interpretation of that much-discussed dictum of Augustine's, and again it is Wessel Gansfort who provides it. But now the reception of Augustine's statement enters a new phase, is seen in a new light, as it functions as the backbone of a treatise specifically dedicated to the question of authority in the church: *Ecclesiastical Dignity and Power: True and Right Obedience.* Wessel's own interpretation, which forms a strong strand running right through his argument, is characteristic of his style of argumentation and his fondness for antithetical formulations:

> . . . For it is, after all, because of God that we believe the gospel, and because of the gospel that we believe in the church and the pope; we do not believe the gospel because of the church.[1]

Wessel's interpretation is almost diametrically opposed to the firm support for ecclesiastical authority that Augustine's statement seems at first sight to suggest. As Wessel has it, the statement refers to the origins of our faith. He goes back to the roots and arrives at God, who is the root of all, the origin of belief in the gospel. All other authorities are subordinate to God and should acknowledge God's supremacy.

In the following subsections, I shall attempt to sketch the context that forms the background to Wessel's short work: it should be read as an elaboration of his interpretation of Augustine's statement.

1. See /759/ below.

27

Violated Trust

The author's plan is not to construct a wide-ranging abstract argument about the authority of the church, but rather to discuss the behavior of those in authority *within* that church: its pope, prelates, *pastores*, and *doctores*. He puts them firmly in their place, and though he does not belittle them, he certainly takes them down a peg or two. The author's trust in the holders of ecclesiastical authority has been severely shaken. Skepticism and suspicion resonate from every page and can be heard loud and clear even in the opening sentence: "The pope should *believe*."[2] Apparently this is not as self-evident as one might expect. "It is God we serve, not the pope."[3] Again and again we find statements of this kind.[4]

I am not going to rehearse the full litany of all the afflictions that beset the church in the fifteenth century—Avignon, the Western Schism, and later in the century also the decadence of the Renaissance popes, which Wessel Gansfort also lived to see. It is scarcely surprising that a man of his spiritual and intellectual caliber would react as he does. He does not mince his words, but his language remains civil and restrained. His moderate tune was to be replaced by a cacophony of invective during the Reformation and beyond.

The Authority of Jean Gerson

The late-medieval theologian to whom Wessel Gansfort refers most often and most respectfully is *"venerabilis Gerson,"* Jean Gerson, chancellor of the University of Paris.[5] Many of these allusions occur in the current treatise about authority in the church, in which Wessel refers to Gerson's essay about the counsels of perfection, though without ever mentioning the work's title (*De consiliis evangelicis*).[6] The meaning and significance of these counsels, mentioned in the Scriptures, determine the scope of the regulations to which a believer binds himself or herself, and not the other way around. With Gerson, Wessel advocates wise moderation as opposed to blind subservience to the letter of the law.

Another of Gerson's works, however, was even more influential on Wessel Gansfort's writing: Gerson's own very well-known treatise on authority in

2. See /748/ below.
3. See /760/ below.
4. A further example can be found in Wessel Gansfort's treatise *De sacramento poenitentiae*: "For after all, it is God we believe in, not the Catholic Church, not a Latin council, and not the pope" (*Opera*, 779).
5. See /751/ below.
6. See /751–52/, n. 52.

the church, bearing the very similar title *De potestate ecclesiastica*. It dates from 1417, when Chancellor Gerson presented it to the conciliar partriarchs at the Council of Constance on February 6. In its tenth decree it "proclaims and lays down that a general council may also be convened without a pope and that in certain cases the pope may be judged by this council" (*Consideratio decima*).[7]

Did Gerson's treatise about authority in the church influence Wessel Gansfort's views? There can be no doubt whatsoever about the matter. The footnotes to the text will provide ample evidence of this.

But there is another reason for Wessel's intellectual and spiritual affinity with this major figure of the Council of Constance. At this council, the two French theologians Pierre d'Ailly and Jean Gerson defended the followers of the *Devotio moderna*; and Wessel Gansfort was a fervent adherent of this spiritual movement, which was such an important part of the late-medieval religious landscape. This affiliation is in itself vitally important when it comes to understanding his critical treatise about those in authority in the church.

Wessel's Audience

It is among the circles of the *Devotio moderna* and like-minded religious communities, such as the Windesheim Congregation (also founded by Geert Groote[8]), that Wessel Gansfort's readers were to be found; and precisely these readers would have been interested in his discussion about authority and power within the church. Perhaps we might imagine a specific audience, with whom the renowned theologian might have maintained contact and exchanged ideas after his return to the Netherlands (about 1477).

For those who followed in Geert Groote's footsteps and shared his spiritual views, the ascent to God passed through the innermost depths of one's own being, through the heart: "I will pray with my spirit, I will pray with my very soul" (Geert Groote).[9] This internalization of faith was of enormous importance to Gansfort, too. His *Opera* show that he took a professional interest in this form of spirituality, which demonstrates certain elements of mysticism. Though he himself was not a member of the clergy or of a religious community, he was a deeply religious man. He too wished to "journey inwards" and believe with his heart. And after his return to the Low Countries, he chose

---

7. *De potestate ecclesiastica. Oeuvres Complètes*, no. 282, p. 229.
8. M. de Kroon, "Gerard Groote," in Martin Greschat, ed., *Gestalten der Kirchengeschichte* 4, Mittelalter II (Stuttgart, etc., 1983), 234–50; bibliography, 249–50.
9. Op. cit., 241.

to spend most of his time in these religious circles. For the first ten years, he lived near Zwolle in the Windesheim Congregation at Agnietenberg or in the Cistercian Abbey of Aduard; he then moved to Groningen, where he lived in the Old Convent, a community of Tertiary Sisters.[10]

2. WHY DID WESSEL GANSFORT WRITE THIS?

But why did Wessel decide to consign these critical views about the holders of authority within the church to writing? In my view, two factors played a decisive role here.

Wessel's Commitment to the Scriptures

What do the Scriptures actually say about authority in the church, precisely with respect to the lamentable and corrupt image exhibited by those in authority in his day, high and low alike? Gansfort carefully collects Bible texts that almost all refer, directly or indirectly, to "authority." This biblical approach takes him straight to the sources from which the brothers and sisters of the *Devotio moderna* and their sympathizers also took their inspiration. Had people from these circles perhaps asked him what exactly was meant by "harsh" (*dyskolos*) in 1 Peter 2:18,[11] or about the relationship between loving God and loving one's neighbor?[12] Had they perhaps questioned the church's worldly wealth?[13] The prominence of Matthew 23 within Wessel's treatise (quoted virtually in full!) and the author's detailed exegesis of this passage give the impression that this was written in answer to the broad interest of his audience. They were obviously concerned about the question of the extent to which they were bound to obey the prelates of

10. See M. van Rhijn, *Studiën*, 119, and esp. J. van Moolenbroek, "The Correspondence of Wessel Gansfort: An Inventory," DRCH 84 (2004): 3–4. The same author convincingly demonstrates Wessel Gansfort's influence on both the monks and visitors of the Cistercian Abbey of Aduard in "Wessel Gansfort as a Teacher at the Cistercian Abbey of Aduard. The Dismissal of Caesarius of Heisterbach's Dialogus Miraculorum," in Koen Goudriaan, Jaap van Moolenbroek, and Ad Tervoort, eds., *Education and Learning in the Netherlands, 1400–1600* (Leiden, Boston, 2004), 113–32.

11. See /750/ below. Actually, the term used in 1 Pet. 2:18 is *tois skoliois; dyskolos* is found in Matt. 19:23, to which Wessel refers in /750/. Both terms can have the same meaning.

12. See /753-5/ below.

13. See / 750-1/ below.

the church. This question was even incorporated as a subtitle into the heading of the treatise.

Wessel's Particular Audience

Wessel's document is characteristic not only of the author, but also of his audience. It is a well-known fact that in the late Middle Ages such spiritual movements as the Beguines, Beghards, *humiliati*, and Waldensians were critical of the ecclesiastical hierarchy. The Beguines, for instance, elected their own pastor if they thought it necessary to have one. On the other hand, the church hierarchy continuously suspected these Christians of harboring heretical views. As late as the fourteenth century, the Beguines were subjected to bloody persecutions.

Geert Groote managed to steer his foundations clear of difficulties with the church authorities. He never attempted to place himself outside the existing structures, and respected the authorities within the church establishment.[14] This same attitude also prevails among Wessel Gansfort's audience and is their defining characteristic. These are inspired Christians looking for the inner self, striving for spirituality.[15] Taking the Bible as their basis, they search for profundity, authenticity, the meaning of faith. At the same time, however, they respect the existing church structure and do not break with the hierarchy. Groote's followers lived in a monastic environment, but did not take any vows. They lived out the gospel and the counsels of perfection without being formally bound.

This attitude also characterizes the critically minded Wessel Gansfort. He accepts the authority of the church and its pastoral office, but measures it against the standards set by the Bible, resolutely furnishing a scriptural basis for the office of the pastor and the controversial matter of clerical jurisdiction. This was to exercise great significance until well after the Reformation and even—if I am not mistaken—until the present day.

To the long list of subjects related to the term "authority," Wessel in his tract adds some more problematic points, which clearly originated in the circles of his specific audience. I shall note three of them: (1) the counsels of perfection mentioned above,[16] (2) the issue of the "unconditional obedience" exacted by

14. M. de Kroon, "Gerard Groote," in Grescher, *Gestalter* (n. 8), 246–47. "The regulations which the Dutch devout bound themselves to obey gave their piety a conventional form and preserved them from dangerous excesses of fervour" (Johan Huizinga, *The Waning of the Middle Ages* [London, 1976], 174). Cf. R. R. Post, *The Modern Devotion: Confrontation with Reformation and Humanism* (Leiden, 1968), esp. chap. 6, 273–92. "They obey the Roman Church and her prelates" (Post, *Modern Devotion*, 276).
15. Cf. /766/, n. 125. Cf. Post, *Modern Devotion*, chap. 8, 314–42.
16. See /751–53/ below.

fanatical spiritual leaders,[17] and (3) the matter of applying to church authorities for dispensation.[18]

3. EXCURSUS: GANSFORT AND LUTHER

Wessel Gansfort's works did not appear in print until 1521–23, more than thirty years after his death; this marked the beginning of the Dutchman's fame. His *Opera* were published successively in Zwolle, Wittenberg, and Basle.[19] Especially this last edition contributed greatly to Wessel's reputation, an effect reinforced by a letter of recommendation from Martin Luther:

> If I had read this man before, it might appear to my enemies as though Luther derived all his ideas from Wessel, so much do we both breathe the same spirit.[20]

This sounds like a definite overstatement and leaves the reader with many questions. A detailed comparison between Luther's theology and that of Gansfort is unfortunately beyond the scope of this book. Yet there is one obvious point of comparison, and within the context of this study it can hardly be left out of consideration: Martin Luther too addressed Augustine's criticism of Mani's *Epistula fundamenti*, already early in his Reformation activities. The context was his discussion with Johannes Eck in Leipzig in 1519,[21] that is, two years before the publication of Gansfort's *Opera*. This sequence of events strengthens the objective value of this modest touchstone.

Luther is evidently very well acquainted with Augustine's letter against the *Epistula fundamenti*. He sharply criticizes the corrupt version of Augustine's statement (*credere* instead of *movere* in the second sentence) and highlights the importance of the historical context (i.e., Augustine's controversy with the Manicheans). Luther proves to be very much at home in Augustine's works; he alludes to a related text in the *Confessiones* and bases his criticism on the literary style of the church father.[22]

The main question here, however, is, does Luther's interpretation also unmistakably echo Wessel's explanation of Augustine's adage? I shall present two phrases here for the reader's consideration:

17. See /756–57/ below.
18. See /770–71/ below.
19. See C. Augustijn, "Wessel Gansfort's Rise to Celebrity," in *Wessel Gansfort (1419–1489) and the Northern Humanism*, ed. F. Akkerman, G. C. Huisman, and A. J. Vanderjagt (Leiden/New York/Cologne, 1993), 3–22.
20. *Opera*, 854.
21. Luther, *Resolutiones super propositionibus suis Lipsiae disputatis*; WA 2:391–435.
22. Op. cit., 428–32 (*Conclusio XII*).

1. "This dictum [of Augustine's] refers to the origin of faith" (Wessel).[23]
   "For this [Augustine's dictum] one must go back to the source, to the origin" (Luther).[24]
2. "If all people turned aside from their faith, I would still hold firm to the gospel" (Wessel).[25]
   "Would you no longer believe, then, even if the whole world were to turn against the gospel?"(Luther).[26]

Two points of similarity do not amount to much. However, these become significant if one probes the depths of the issues to which they refer.

4. PRELIMINARY REMARKS ON THE PRESENT EDITION OF WESSEL GANSFORT'S TREATISE ON AUTHORITY IN THE CHURCH

The original Latin text of Wessel's tract was not printed exactly flawlessly. Sometimes this is a matter of minor printing errors, but sometimes entire words have been lost. Moreover, this unusual document is characterized by an unusual style: forceful, plain, and succinct, with no beating about the bush. In the text-critical notes to the Latin text below, I point out major printing errors and grammatical or syntactical problems. The *marginalia* are also included in the notes.

The real problems, however, do not relate so much to the transmission of the text as to the document's context. Who or what exactly is the target of Wessel's critical argument? What is he alluding to at a given time? These things are not always clear. The edition of his tract opens up a rich source, but more research is needed if we are to enjoy its full flow.

When reading the document, the reader will inevitably be struck by Wessel's vast erudition in the important academic disciplines of his day, especially theology and both canon and secular law. Wessel also clearly takes a great interest in medicine and the work of physicians.[27]

Most of Wessel's *Opera* have been translated into English,[28] including his tract *De dignitate et potestate ecclesiastica*. However, in Miller's 1917 edition, the

---

23. *Opera*, 893.
24. Luther, *Resolutiones*, 430, 13–14.
25. *Opera*, 893.
26. Luther, *Resolutiones*, 431, 21–22.
27. Van Rhijn, *Studiën*, 103–7.
28. *Wessel Gansfort: Life and Writings*, by Edward Waite Miller, D.D., *Principal Works*, trans. Jared Waterbury Scudder, M.A., 2 vols. (New York and London, 1917). Cf. Van Rhijn, *Studiën*, 179–85.

original Latin text is not provided, and there are no text-critical or explanatory notes.

5. WESSEL GANSFORT, *ECCLESIASTICAL DIGNITY AND POWER*

Of true and right obedience. To what extent are we bound to obey the commandments and statutes of the leaders of the church?[a]

We are not bound to believe what the pope says unless he believes in a right manner

The pope must *believe*; this obligation binds him just as it binds all believers. And as long as he believes as he should, the faithful are obliged to believe what he believes: not because *he* believes it, but because he believes what he ought to believe. If, however, another person's faith is truer than the pope's, then the pope himself ought to bring his faith in line with that person's, be this a layman or even a woman: not *because* it is a layman or a woman who believes in this way, but because this person has set off along the right path toward the truth of the gospel.

Take the case of Peter, for example (see Gal. 2 [11–14]). Peter did not approach the gospel in the right manner. For this reason he had to be guided by Paul: not because of who Paul was, or because he was subordinate to Paul, but because the latter approached the truth of the gospel better. Hence the conclusion: *It may be assumed that the pope and prelates have come to understand the truth of the gospel better as they have risen above all others in rank and dignity. And for this reason, all things being equal, we should be more ready to believe them than merely one of their subjects. Nevertheless, their subjects are not simply bound to believe them.* For sometimes this is so completely unreasonable, or so full of blasphemy, that it can be more pernicious than any heresy whatsoever. Any prelate, even the highest prelate, may err, just as the first of them erred, even though he was personally selected by our Lord Jesus himself, and was filled with the Holy Spirit.[29] But this happened, and the Lord permitted it to happen.

a. The text-critical notes consist of suggestions, additions, and corrections to the Latin text. The text is a faithful reproduction of the edition of *Opera* (1614).
NOTE:
   scl., *scilicet* = to wit, namely
   i.e., *id est* = that is to say
   add., *addendum* = add/supply . . .
   corr., *corrigendum* = correct as . . .
   marg., *in margine* = in the margin
29. Cf. Acts 4:8.

We should know that our faith is due not to a human being, but to the Holy Spirit. And rightly so. For since faith is a theological virtue dedicated solely to God, it believes in God alone; and in God alone can the just live by faith.[30] Indeed the life of the just man would be severely endangered if it were dependent on the life of the pope, for many of the highest pontiffs have erred disastrously.

This has been revealed in our own days at the celebrated Council of Constance. Benedict [XIII], Boniface [IX] and John XXIII /749/ have all gravely damaged the faith![31] And then, latterly, we have Pius II and Sixtus IV—the former bought himself the kingdoms of the earth in open bulls,[32] and the other abused his apostolic authority by issuing sealed bulls, in the fullness of his power, to grant the most shameful of dispensations, not only in relation to an oath taken in civil law proceedings, but also in relation to an oath yet to be taken. All that Brother Pietro or his fellow Girolamo had done, driven by insolence or greed, this pope ratified later, on learning of their doings, and here too with sealed bulls.[33]

30. Cf. Rom. 3:28.

31. Of the three popes named, both Benedict XIII (pope in Avignon from 1394) and John XXIII (elected in Pisa in 1409) were deposed at the Council of Constance in 1417. Wesssel does not mention the contender for the papacy in Rome, Gregory XII, who stepped down voluntarily. Who does get a mention from this rival camp is Gregory's predecessor, Boniface IX, who was infamous for his avarice, simony, and lively trade in jubilee indulgences.

32. Pius II (1458–64), Enea Silvio de' Piccolomini, acquired significant influence from 1431 as the secretary of several conciliar fathers at the Council of Basle. He allied himself with the camp opposing Eugene IV, holding the council to be superior to the pope. Once he himself became pope, he set aside his former frivolous ways (in his famous admonition to "Reject Aeneas, embrace Pius") and emerged as a fierce opponent of conciliar theory. In his bull *Execrabilis* (1460), he condemned the practice of appealing to a general council against the pope of Rome. Indirectly this bull was also directed against the Pragmatic Sanction of Bourges (1438). This sanction attempted to put the Council of Basle into practice by elevating the council's decrees to the status of law, which had enormous consequences—both financial and otherwise—for the pope's temporal powers in France. A similar move had occurred in Germany in 1439. This is what Wessel Gansfort is alluding to here, thus indirectly revealing himself to be an adherent of conciliar theory. See L. von Pastor, *Geschichte der Päpste im Zeitalter der Renaissance von der Thronbesteigung Pius' II bis zum Tode Sixtus' IV*, vol. 2 (Freiburg [Br.], 1925), 5–289, esp. 103–64.

33. The brothers Girolamo and Cardinal Pietro Riario were the evil genius behind the papacy of the Renaissance pope Sixtus IV (1471–84). Since Gansfort uses a legal term (*ratificavit*), it is possible that he is here alluding to the machinations by which Pietro Riario maneuvered his brother Girolamo toward an advantageous marriage into the nobility. See von Pastor, *Geschichte*, 488f. When this plan failed in its first incarnation, the intended bride was promptly set aside to make way for another. All of this maneuvering was later crowned with the blessing of Sixtus IV. See von Pastor, *Geschichte*, no.113. But Wessel's statement comprises a much more serious accusation. Evidently

Peter, the first pope, erred and was corrected by Paul as an example to all, so that the wise might know what they should do with salt that has lost its taste.[34]

No pope could be wiser than Peter; none could have more authority than St. Peter; none could be holier that St. Peter. And if one has no right to ask the pope, "why do you do it this way?" or to censure or judge a pope, one ought least of all to censure Peter. But, I ask, what if the pope is censurable, and does not approach the truth of the gospel in the right way? If this is plain to see for all who are filled with the Spirit of God's wisdom, why should he not be censured by that same Spirit? The wisest and saintliest of them all was publicly censured—in the presence of all—by one who was even wiser, even more saintly: what humiliation![35] Paul reproached him after the gift of the Holy Spirit, just as, before the gift of the Holy Spirit, our Lord Jesus upbraided the eleven as they reclined at table.[36]

Paul reproached Peter for his fear, human weakness, and inconstancy, and for being a stumbling block for the faithful, not only the simple-hearted, but also the righteous, such as the apostle Barnabas.[37] And this he did to Peter's ignominy and public shame. Since this happened to Peter with divine approval, God's goodness was acting not only in relation to Peter, but in relation to the whole church, to strengthen it in every age.

All these negative factors, however, prompted Peter to make a stronger and more successful comeback after his ruin: with love, wisdom, and humility. And from Paul all the wise can learn what they should do with the salt of the earth if it should threaten to lose its taste. For it is no longer good for anything other than to be thrown out, to be trampled underfoot by those who are

---

he regards Pope Sixtus IV as an accomplice to the murder of Giuliano de Medici (on April 26, 1478). Cf. von Pastor, *Geschichte*, 532–41. The sealed bulls mentioned at the end of this passage refer to the excommunication imposed on Lorenzo de Medici and his followers because of their violent reaction to the assassination. The city of Florence was placed under an interdict (von Pastor, *Geschichte*, 542f.). The Italian historian Marcello Simonetta has recently established that Sixtus IV did indeed plan to eliminate Lorenzo de Medici (*Trouw* newspaper, Mar. 2, 2004, 12).

34. Cf. Matt. 5:13. In this section, opening with the image of the salt that has lost its taste, Wessel raises the issue of whether a pope who "abuses the gospel" should be called to account. This thorny issue also made its mark in the *Decretum Gratiani*. See canon *Si Papa* (Distinctio XL): "The pope may not be judged by anybody, unless he is censured for deviating from the faith" *(. . . nisi deprehendatur a fide devius)*. Cf. also the canon *Nos si incompetenter* (Causa II, Quaestio VII), which states that criticism can be necessary, as otherwise we will be "masters of error above all the others" *(erimus prae ceteris erroris magistri)*.

35. Cf. Gal. 2:14.
36. Cf. Mark 16:14.
37. Cf. Gal. 2:13.

wiser.[38] But only insofar as it has lost its taste, no more. This principle is of eminent significance with a view to prelates of the church who are unworthy. /750/

We must obey our masters, even the harsh ones. What does this mean?

The word *dyscolis* in the canonical Epistle of St. Peter—"Slaves, accept the authority of your masters with all deference, not only those who are kind and gentle but also those who are harsh"[39]—is not so binding on slaves as many would believe. For many interpret the position of the slave as though he were bound to follow all the orders of bad masters. But these people do not understand the full force of the Greek word. For *dyscolos* means "difficult to attain," as it is used in Matthew 19 [:23]: "It will be hard for a rich person to enter the kingdom of heaven." We must obey harsh masters, not bad ones, that is, not those who command us to do wrong.

How should we interpret the statutes of the prelates of the church? When should we accept their leadership, and when should we reject it?

When the Pharisees asked the Lord why his disciples broke the tradition of the elders,[40] he responded with a more important question, which is extremely instructive for us. For here our Lord teaches us both by his word and by his example. By his word: we should know that the statutes of the prelates of the church should not be understood as God's commandments—for that would mean that the yoke of the gospel would carry more weight than the yoke of the law.[41] He also teaches us, by his example, that the faithful must react and protest if ever they discern that their superiors have made a scandalous error. If this error is still secret, they should do so secretly, and if it is out in the open, they should protest openly.[42] For the Lord countered their attempts to thwart him by holding up their errors before them. And rightly so, as otherwise their arrogance—already boundless and dependent on their own whims—would become still greater, and would then be impossible to censure, restrain, or check.

Therefore, if ever they sin shamelessly, and insolently persist in their sin—for lack of moderation always goes hand in hand with such behavior—they must be called to order according to the example of the Lord. However, take heed that they are admonished in a salutary manner, as otherwise the word of

38. Cf. Matt. 5:13.
39. Cf. 1 Pet. 2:18; cf. n. 11.
40. Matt. 15:2ff.
41. Matt. 11:29–30. For Wessel's view of the relationship between the gospel and the law, see /758-59/ and n. 90.
42. Cf. Matt. 18:15–18.

the Lord will be cast aside in contempt. For as long as they sit on Moses' seat, we must do as they say.[43] And they may be considered to occupy that seat as long as their words are not openly in conflict with their deeds. But if their life is so scandalous that they corrupt more by their example than they edify by their words—from that moment on, they cannot be tolerated. For then they do not sit in the seat of Peter, but the seat of scoffers.[44] The Lord provides an example for all this. He removes them from office. Thus all these people, useless as they are, must be cast out in order to prevent even greater turpitude.

/751/ Is it both good and bad for the Church to possess riches?

1. It is good that the church has great riches and temporal power. And it would be better still if she had even more. For it is a good thing to be able to do many good works, and it would be better to be able to do still more.

2. It is bad that the church has great riches and temporal power—not only because bad could come of it, but because a great deal of bad has indeed come of it. The bishops of old made a big mistake in assuming jurisdiction[45] and thus admitting wealth. For the secular princes want to provide for their own from the wealth of the church,[46] and they are nearly all corrupt. And those who are honest when they are taken on are corrupted by the pressures of the position and their many cares.

---

43. Cf. Matt. 23:2–3.

44. Cf. Ps. 1:1 (*cathedra pestilentiae* is an echo of the Vulgate).

45. The Latin text uses the term *judiciaria*. See J. F. Niermeyer, *Mediae latinitatis lexicon minus*, rev. ed. (Leiden, Boston, 2002), 740ff. Several *novellas* (535–65) of the *Corpus Iuris Civilis* still impose restrictions on the jurisdiction of bishops. Cf. M. de Kroon, *Studien zu Martin Bucers Obrigkeitsverständnis. Evangelisches Ethos und politisches Engagement* (Gütersloh, 1984), 102–5.
The question of the wealth of the church is reminiscent of the conflict concerning evangelical poverty that the pope in Avignon, John XXII (1316–34)—himself a notable canonist—battled out with sympathizers of Francis of Assisi. This context calls up the association with the legislation enacted by this pope on the matter in question. See CIC Extravagantes, de Verborum significatione, Tit. XIV, Cap. III, *Ad conditorem canonum*, and Cap. IV, *Cum inter nonnullos*. However, the fact that wealth was assigned a fixed place within the church, with a firm legal basis, can be understood only against the background of the privileged status that the clergy had gradually acquired over the centuries. Finally, at the Lateran Councils of 1179 and 1215, the church demanded tax-free status for its clergy and for ecclesiastical possessions. The legal aspects of this immunity are worked out in detail in the *Decretals* of Gregory IX (1227–41) and in *Liber VI* of Boniface VIII (1294–1303). Wessel Gansfort's fascinating analysis reveals that he views these developments in a negative light. Wealth corrupts. The subsequent theme, simony, is closely connected with this.

46. Ecclesiastical wealth serving profane interests! An apt description can be found in F. Rapp, *Réformes et Réformation à Strasbourg. Église et société dans le diocèse de Strasbourg (1450–1525)* (Paris [1974]), 281–318.

Simony and the granting of benefices—does the pope do well to take on this task?

No matter whether someone who has obtained a [benefice] also practices simony[47]—by acquiring or taking that benefice—he is not the owner.[48] This means that canons do not own benefices[49] or their proceeds, so they cannot give them away. The pope cannot give them away either, nor can he sell them. The only right he can transfer [regarding these benefices] is that of administering them in good faith. He can transfer this right, and can entrust it to those who will administer it in good faith. But nobody, not even the pope, is permitted to tolerate these benefices being administered in bad faith, unless to avert a worse evil that would otherwise certainly follow. And anything else carried out in relation to benefices is not legally binding. By making the granting of benefices his own business, what is the pope doing but increasing the onus on him to account for what he does?[50]

If, however, he shares out remunerations or revenues[51] (or anything of that kind) to dissolute or corrupt people, he is not dispensing them for the sake of the divine office. And since when it comes to assigning responsibility over ecclesiastical possessions in faraway places, possessions intended for the divine office, he simply trusts to luck (almost as though he could not care less), it is sadly impossible for him to see with his own eyes the evils which ensue.

47. Simony, trading in spiritual goods, has always been subject to the curse that Peter uttered over Simon the magician (Acts 8:9ff.). But it seems that simony is difficult to stamp out. Canon law did not succeed in banishing it (see Decr. Gregorius IX, Lib. V, Tit. III, *De simonia*), nor did the theological arguments presented by Jean Gerson at the Council of Constance. See Gerson, *Tractatus de simonia*, in *Oeuvres Complètes*, no. 276 (Oct. 1415) and *Ad reformationem contra simoniam*, op. cit., no. 279 (June 1416).

48. This theme is treated repeatedly in the final books of the CIC (the *Clementinen* and the *Extravagantes Communes*) under the heading *De rebus ecclesiae non alienandis*.

49. A benefice is an ecclesiastical position that entails a fixed income. Cf. *Codex Juris Canonici, Can. 1409*.

50. Gerson expresses the same criticism. He believes that the pope meddles too much with ecclesiastical property: "against the natural course of affairs, the head usurps everything that the limbs could each handle for themselves" (*De potestate ecclesiastica, Oeuvres Complètes*, no. 282, p. 239).

51. *Servitia (communia)* are a form of tax imposed by the popes from the thirteenth or fourteenth century on granting the higher benefices (such as bishoprics, abbeys, etc.). Wessel does not make clear precisely what abuses he is alluding to here. See also Niermeyer, *Mediae* (n. 45), 1259f. However, the use of the term *distrahere* (here translated as "to share out") shows that the pope could forgo these revenues for the sake of other, political goals: simony in practice. This tax system led directly to simony— "inevitably," in Gerson's eyes.

To what extent the statutes and commandments of men are mandatory

The admirable Gerson has amply demonstrated to what extent regulations concerning the hours and fasting are mandatory.[52] That which is alleged about the most reasonable wisdom they contain does not detract from this, because *that* is not where the danger of these obligations lies.

And the same is true of the counsels of perfection. They contain a wealth of wisdom. Nevertheless, God did not wish to oblige the weak (who make up the majority) to keep these counsels, though they must keep what the counsels ultimately signify. /752/ For ultimately, of course, nobody will enter [the kingdom of heaven] other than through the eye of the needle,[53] like a dove through a cleft of the rock.[54]

Therefore, the reason adduced means that the precepts of the prelates in the church are mandatory insofar as they reveal wisdom. To which I add: they are mandatory on the condition that they actually deliver up the fruit they bear.[55] For if all those who are less strong are permitted—without committing a deadly sin—not to attain all the perfections of the counsels of perfection and still to be children of light,[56] who would want to set all these weak people a deadly snare?[57] For surely this goes further than the essential commandments demand? For this reason I wonder greatly about people who wish to make an obligation of an admonition.

For surely all power within the church is like an agreement between a physician and a person who is ill. That is to say, it consists of an agreement between two parties.[58] For a pastor can be a shepherd only insofar as he

52. In his *De consiliis evangelicis* (*Opera omnia*, ed. L. Du Pin [Antwerp, 1706], 2:669–81), Jean Gerson discusses not only the classical counsels of perfection, but also the hours (here called *vigiliae*) and practices relating to fasting. Gerson places the counsels of perfection in their correct context: the perfection of the Christian way of life does not lie in these counsels, but rather in love itself (op. cit., 669–70). He also distinguishes clearly between the counsels and the commandments: the latter are essential for a Christian life, whereas the counsels are merely instrumental. As Gerson puts it, "I conclude: the incumbency of the commandments is more important and more far-reaching than that of the [monastic] vows" (op. cit., 677).

53. Cf. Mark 10:25.

54. Cf. Song 2:14.

55. As much as he can, Gansfort weakens the obligation entailed in espousing the counsels of perfection (through vows, *vota*). For these are merely the precepts of the church, and can thus never attain the absolute validity reserved for God's commandments. The danger that these *vota* (vows) may be viewed as God-given commandments is always present.

56. Luke 16:8.

57. 1 Tim. 3:7.

58. This view of authority within the church as an agreement between two parties is characteristic of Wessel Gansfort. He elaborates this idea in more detail in /765–66/, see below, n. 143. For the following, cf. Matt. 16:19.

shepherds his flock; he cannot save except insofar as his sheep are saved; he cannot bind except insofar as they are bound with the bonds of love; he cannot unbind them except insofar as they are unbound from the bonds of Satan.

The church received this power from her Lord. If the one faithfully fulfills his office, and the other is faithfully obedient, then both will receive the fruits of their labors. Power in the church is contingent on the extent to which it feeds the flock. It is also a power that lies in reciprocity: the one can provide food only to the extent that the other will be fed.

A counsel to the weak

[The pastor] acts strongly for the weak, not only where there is a danger of sexual incontinency, as the apostle puts it: "But because of cases of sexual immorality, each man should have his own wife and each woman her own husband. For it is better to marry than to be aflame with passion."[59] And further: "Do not deprive one another except perhaps by agreement for a set time, to devote yourselves to prayer, and then come together again, so that Satan may not tempt you because of your lack of self-control."[60]

But even if there are good reasons to fear other temptations—such as irresoluteness, impatience, or inconstancy—it would equally be wise to humbly accept lower aspirations. For most people "it is vain to rise up early."[61] But "stay in the city," your eyes fixed on the Lord, until we "have been clothed in power from on high."[62]

And here there arises the grave question: are any of these weak people actually permitted to throw the counsel of the apostle to the winds? And is a rejection of this kind so irrevocable that one cannot later take the apostle's counsel to heart after all? I believe that a foolish promise displeases God, just as irresponsible oaths do not bind anyone to do things that will oppose his salvation. /753/ For the apostle says: "But if they are not practicing self-control, they should marry."[63] And it is with an eye to the irresoluteness of the weak that our Lord Jesus says "when they persecute you in one town, flee to the next."[64] So strongly does the advice given to the weak signify their path to salvation, that everything that does not stand in the way of that salvation is beneficial to it. As it is said: "Whoever is not against you is for you."[65]

59. 1 Cor. 7:2a and 9b.
60. 1 Cor. 7:5.
61. Ps. 127:2.
62. Luke 24:49.
63. 1 Cor. 7:9.
64. Matt. 10:23.
65. Luke 9:50.

A pastor is appointed to graze the Lord's flock. But because the flock to be grazed is in possession of reason and free will, it is not entirely delivered into the power of the pastor. Then the flock would have no other obligation than to obey the pastor. But the sheep must determine for themselves by whom they will be grazed, by whom they may be infected, and how a fatal infection—even if caused by the pastor himself—is to be avoided. And there would be no excuse of these sheep if they followed the pastor.

Thus people should follow their pastors to the pastures. But if a pastor does not graze his sheep, he is not a pastor; nor is the flock obliged to follow him, since he is then not properly in office. For sometimes a good pastor demands what is right, in the right way, and then we must obey him. Sometimes he demands something that is in itself correct, but demands this in an incorrect manner, and then, too, we should obey him as usual, as in: "Do what they say, but not what they do . . . etc."[66] But if, purely through ignorance and with the best possible intentions, a good pastor commands something that is wrong, while the flock knows better, they should not obey him. This applies all the more if the pastor commands something that is not right and does so, moreover, in a manner that is not right.

Loving my neighbor is my debt to God, not to my neighbor

I have been commanded to love my neighbor.[67] Therefore it is not to my neighbor that I owe this love of my neighbor, for it is not my neighbor who, by putting me under an obligation by his law, made me a debtor. I owe this debt to God alone. He alone put me under an obligation by his law. From this it is immediately clear how true the words of the repentant man are in the psalm: "Against you, you alone, have I sinned."[68]

Yet we are said to owe loyalty, reverence, respect, gratitude, obedience [to others]. In the Our Father, our Lord says that some people are our debtors.[69] And the apostle admonishes us: "Owe no one anything, other than to love one another,"[70] as though this, at least, should be recognized as a debt, that we should love one another. But since it is impossible for one truth to contradict

66. Cf. Matt. 23:3.
67. Cf. Luke 10:27. In the solution that Wessel offers here, he tries to alleviate the apparent opposition between the two components in the section heading. At the same time, his exposition of the highest commandment of love provides a striking example of his use of antithetical formulations: "our duty to God, not to our neighbor." Cf. also /770/, where he also presents two statements that seem to contradict one another, though there in the context of the ethical issue of *perplexitas*, where choosing in favor of one or the other leads to problems. See /770–71/ below.
68. Ps. 51:4.
69. Cf. Matt. 6:12.
70. Rom. 13:8.

another,[71] and the two above-mentioned statements both stand incontrovert-ibly, the latter two must be interpreted thus: that they reveal a healthy and true principle. /754/

Therefore to angels and prelates we owe reverence;[72] to our parents loy-alty, to benefactors gratitude, and to the needy assistance, insofar as this can reasonably and beneficially be bestowed. Not because we owe it to them, but because what we owe to God, who commands us thus, benefits those whom we help. Hence this manner of speaking has more than one meaning, it is not unequivocal; it is a pithy saying, whose meaning is not immediately clear. The two commandments, to love God and to love one's neighbor,[73] are God's commandments and are obligatory by reason of his will. All the command-ments of the law simply make us debtors to God. Therefore it is not to man that I owe a debt not to kill, hate, or slander him, because it was not man who imposed this law on man, or obligated him by a law. No law, whether it was passed by the common consent of the people or by prelates, princes, or mag-istrates, is more obligatory for anyone than is expressed or enjoined in divine law. In the divine law we are commanded to obey those in authority, not to put up resistance to the authorities, to respect public order in our towns, and many other such things, which cannot be maintained without these laws. Therefore we ought to obey them. We do not, however, owe that obedience itself to them. We owe it to God to obey them, just as we owe it to God, not to them, to love them.

From this perspective it now becomes clearer how we should obey the com-mands of those in authority. Since we owe it to God to obey them, we should obey them insofar as they do not command anything that goes against God; for nothing should be done for the sake of God that goes against God. From this perspective it is also easily apparent *how far* they may go in their commands, and *what sort* of commands they may be. The conscience must be aware of both these perspectives. It is a different matter when it comes to an obligation in the secular or civil-law sphere. In this area, the obligation holds only to the

---

71. According to a principle of Greek philosophy, *because that which is true must concur with itself in every respect*. Aristotle, *Analytica priora* 32, 37a, r.8–9 (δεῖ γὰρ πᾶν τὸ ἀληθὲς αὐτὸ ἑαυτῷ ὁμολογούμενον εἶναι πάντῃ).

72. An extremely concise reference to Dionysius the Areopagite (Pseudo-Dionysius, late fifth/early sixth century), specifically to his writings *De coelesti hierarchia* and *De ecclesiastica hierarchia*, which had an indelible influence on medieval theology. The hierarchical structure of the heavenly bodies, "the choirs of angels," whose ranks gradually ascend to God, is reflected in the hierarchy within the church. Gerson refers to these ideas approvingly in his *De potestate ecclesiastica* (*Oeuvres Complètes*, no. 282, pp. 219–27). Wessel Gansfort is a great deal more critical. See /752/ above, and /765/ below, esp. n. 143.

73. Cf. Luke 10:27.

extent that a good command creates a bond that one accepts willingly and that meets with one's expectations. For example: a patient is obliged to listen to his doctor, but only insofar as he expects the doctor's instructions to be fruitful for good health. If the results are great, the obligation to listen to the doctor is great; if the results are scant, there is scant obligation to listen. And the obligation is scant, equally, to obey a doctor whom one knows to be foolish.

Thus one is always under an obligation to obey a command if one expects good to come of keeping it. For cases of this kind, the following rule holds: You are not bound by a command if greater harm will come of keeping it than of disregarding it or dismissing it.[74] /755/ It is right, then, that schoolmasters' commands are disregarded and ignored by children who are poor. For them it is a bitter necessity to earn money in order to live. This is more important than to receive schooling and make a glorious career. For if they were to attend school, they would have to pay for this with their health and their life. If they do not obey, their punishment is that they cannot speak grammatically, with all that that entails. The same applies to the rules of logic and of philosophy, and to the commands of kings and of popes. For where salvation is concerned, one should obey the pope in the same manner as one would a doctor if one were ill, as long as one can form a proper judgment about the instructions of these two. And anyone who is not capable of forming a proper judgment, if he is in doubt, should rely on the guidance of someone he trusts completely.

How far prelates must be obeyed by those who are subject to them

Most of those in authority over churches and monasteries demand prompt obedience, even measured against the guidelines provided by the sacred Scriptures. This obedience is necessary for those under their authority to achieve salvation, as it is written: "Do whatever they teach you and follow it; but do not do as they do."[75] But let us inspect this obedience accurately, both in terms of the intentions of the person giving the command and in terms of the command itself, in terms of the necessity of the command, but also of its

---

74. It is not clear whether this is a quotation, though the text is italicized in the edition. Perhaps Wessel is simply summing up and emphasizing what has gone before. The thinking behind the summary is well known: it is derived from Aristotle's legal philosophy, where it is indicated by the term ἐπιείκεια (*Ethica Nicomachea* 5, p. 14; 1137a–38a). This expression refers to "better justice," an improvement on codified law, which can never "do justice" to every concrete case. "If the legislator were present, or another sensible person were to be asked, in a specific case he would make an exception to the general rule," as Jean Gerson puts it in *De potestate ecclesiastica* (*Oeuvres Complètes*, no. 282, p. 230). In addition to the term *epieikeia*, Gerson also uses the words *interpretatio, dispensatio,* "good faith," and "equity" to refer to these exceptions (ibid.).

75. Matt. 23:3.

result and purpose. For it was God's will that the simple, inexperienced people would be provided with advice through the wisdom of the person in authority, which would help them to ascend to God. It was because he wished the simple people to share in his wisdom that God imposed obligations on them.

But it is not only wisdom that will be the fruit of those who obey faithfully, since prompt and humble obedience is a good thing in itself; unless, of course, it would be completely foolish to obey, so foolish that there would be no room at all for the prudence of the serpent.[76] One should not listen to a prelate unless there is wisdom in what he says. For whoever listens to the leaders of the church after the apostles is listening to Christ.[77] If they teach or issue instructions in accordance with Christ, one must listen to them as though wisdom itself were speaking. In other cases one should not listen to them, just as Paul did not listen to Peter when he tried to impose Jewish customs on the Gentiles by his improper example.[78] In all things, therefore, which express wisdom, we must listen [to those in authority in the church] as though Wisdom were speaking from heaven, precisely due to the wisdom contained in their words.[79] It is not, therefore, simply because of their authority as a pastor that we should listen to them. Their canons and statutes have only as much force as they contain wisdom. For this reason, the ecclesiastical authorities cannot impose commands under pain of mortal sin, /756/ unless the transgression of the disobedient person in itself comprises mortal stupidity. This means that in neutral matters—such as Pope Pius [II]'s decree *De alumina*, for instance—the faithful cannot be placed under an obligation on pain of mortal sin simply because a pope so decides.[80]

Explication of the words of our Lord about heeding the scribes and the Pharisees. How should we interpret what he says?

The saying of the Lord Jesus about the Pharisees and scribes sitting in Moses's seat will have to be observed in all its implications, if we consider it with a

76. Cf. Matt. 10:16.
77. Cf. Luke 10:16.
78. Cf. Gal. 2:11–14.
79. It is noteworthy that the term "wisdom" plays a major role in Wessel's critical thinking. This is particularly striking in the current passage. The author is apparently deeply convinced of the wisdom of Jesus ben Sira: "All wisdom is from the Lord" (Sir. 1:1). See also /766-67/ below.
80. Again Wessel expresses criticism of Pius II (d. 1464) (cf. n. 32 above). The pope viewed the discovery of the alum mines in Tolfa (probably in 1462) as a gift from God and earmarked the profit for Christendom's struggle against the Turks. In his decree *De alumine*, Christians are urged to buy this mineral exclusively from Rome, no longer from the enemies of the faith. Wessel is very succinct in his formulation of the obligation imposed on the faithful by the papal decree, but his meaning is clear. Cf. von Pastor, *Geschichte* (n. 32), 236–37.

careful eye, even if this may cause irritation to those who talk about it without due reflection. For if we consider the full implications of this command, it is sufficiently delineated and defined.[81] And this holds in a twofold sense: it is delineated, firstly, by that which went before, that is, those "who sit on Moses's seat," which means those who teach in accordance with Moses. And secondly, it is delineated by what follows at the end, where it is said, "Do not as they do, for they do not practice what they teach." This also constitutes a considerable restriction. Because if we are not allowed to do as they do—even if they had become so shameless as to teach and speak in accordance with their deeds—they would no longer be allowed to be accepted and listened to. And nor would it be possible to excuse anyone who obeyed their words (which correspond to their deeds), however broadly the Lord Jesus says, "Do whatever they teach you." For people who say these sorts of things do not sit on the seat of Moses, but in the seat of pestilence,[82] since they do not speak as did Moses, whose words were inspired by the Holy Spirit. Yet even corrupt men may speak in accordance with Moses, even if they do not think as he did, just as a dead book may direct a living person. A dead statute book must be read, and the same holds for the words of a dead scribe or a dead Pharisee.

The apostle enjoins us to "test everything" and to "hold fast to what is good."[83] So whatever they tell us to do, not in accordance with their own corrupt inclination, but in accordance with the correct teaching of Moses—these things we must do and observe. Otherwise we are not obliged to do or observe what they say.

True and right obedience

If obedience is put into practice properly, it is part of natural justice.[84] For after all, a subject must always obey a just order given by a superior. For this reason, /757/ the commandments of the commanding God must always be obeyed, since they are always just. But obeying the commands of others indiscriminately shows a lack of discretion. The apostle says that we should not even obey the commands of the angels in heaven if they herald and proclaim something other than they were entrusted with.[85]

Everyone who issues commands wishes to be obeyed, but not everyone is guided by the same spirit. A virtuous prelate demands obedience because

81. For the following, cf. Matt. 23:2–3, and /759/ below.
82. Cf. Ps. 1:1 (*cathedra pestilentiae*, see n. 44 above).
83. 1 Thess. 5:21.
84. Cf. Thomas Aquinas, *Summa theologiae* 2.2, q.4, a.7, ad 3: "Obedience has the quality of an obligation that one must fulfill. Seen in that light, it is a special virtue and a part of justice." Cf. also op. cit., q.104, a.2, ad 2.
85. Cf. Gal. 1:8.

he believes that it will be in the best interests of the person who obeys him. A corrupt prelate demands obedience from his subjects so that he may rule however he fancies. Some people, who do not discern the difference, state recklessly and fanatically that one must always obey. Even if there were not a single positive aspect to be found to it, this unconditional obedience would have the sufficient result that it would deny one's own will—as though denying one's own will were always a good thing! In this they quote the words of St Bernard: "Nothing will burn in hell, if not one's own will."[86] But these people do not realize that everyone's will is to be broken there. So breaking someone's will is not always good for that person, unless their more deep-seated will remains unbroken.

Some people, however, assert that disobedience disrupts and damages the peace in monasteries and churches, thus also damaging love, and that love must always be preserved, meaning that one must always be obedient.[87] If these people were to think more carefully about the meaning of the word "love," they would not make such hasty assertions about unconditional obedience.

There is love of God and love of one's neighbor. When it comes to loving people, one should always bear in mind that the thing that is most beneficial should be loved the most. And to such an extent that sometimes the lesser good must be discarded and dispensed with for the sake of the greater good. One should always strive for good brotherly relations if they can be maintained in brotherly love. But if love is endangered, the temporary good relations within the household must be cast aside, just as grain is cast overboard in a storm. After all, one cannot live on good terms with those who err, with underhanded, unsavory characters, with the godless. "For what fellowship is there between light and darkness?"[88] Therefore we should not always obey

86. This statement does not occur in so many words in Bernard of Clairvaux's treatise *De gratia et libero arbitrio*; MSL 182, p. 1001–30 (written in 1127). However, in terms of content, Wessel's statement does concur with what Bernard says. In his treatise, Bernard distinguishes three kinds of freedom: (1) freedom of will, in which lies the true likeness between God and humanity; (2) freedom of deliberation; (3) freedom of agreement. The latter two types of freedom are lost through sin and damnation. The first type of freedom, true freedom of will, is unassailable: "It never deviates in the slightest from the state in which it was created; rather, whether in heaven, on earth, or in hell, it is always the same, as is in accordance with its nature" (cap. IX, p. 30; op. cit., 1017B; English after the Dutch translation of Anton van Duinkerken).

87. Wessel Gansfort is here alluding to the topic of evangelical obedience, one of the counsels of perfection, which in ecclesiastical and monastic circles is espoused with a solemn vow. Scripture does not contain any clear statements on this matter, but evidently this way of life—characterized by absolute obedience—led to misconceptions and mistakes. Wessel highlights the supremacy of love, which is very much reminiscent of Jean Gerson's treatise *De consiliis evangelicis*. See above, n. 52, p. 669–72.

88. 2 Cor. 6:14. For the previous image of lightening the ship's load in a storm, cf. Acts 27:38.

anyone who issues orders merely for the sake of preserving the peace or denying one's own will. /758/

*How should we understand the statement "Accept the authority of every
human institution"?*

Peter says: "For the Lord's sake, accept the authority of every human institution."[89] He understands this statement primarily with reference to spiritual
leaders. For the common believers should be subject to their superiors by
believing their teaching, and by obeying their commands. But in so doing,
they should remain aware that it is for God's sake that they are obliged to do
this. This means that they must fix their faith first and foremost on God and
on the gospel. They offer up their obedience first and foremost to God.

When, therefore, the people believe their pastor—if it is a matter of faith,
in any case—they believe him because his belief is in accordance with the
gospel. And if they believe that the pastor is not preaching in accordance with
the gospel, they should not believe him, and equally they should not obey
him if he gives commands that are contrary to the law. This is what is meant
by accepting the authority of every human institution for the Lord's sake:
believing the pastor for the sake of the gospel and obeying his commands and
following his example because of the law.[90]

The gospel contains the truth, the law the commandments and the great
example for us to follow,[91] to know how we are to obey the words of the gospel and comply with the precepts of the law. This makes it patently clear to
what extent a *doctor theologiae*, by virtue of his office, is to be subject, in matters
of faith, to what a prelate believes. For if he is truly a teacher, well informed
and professional as he should be, he ought, since he is well trained in his art,
to know the truths of the holy Scriptures as well as, or better than, those
who are not teachers, that is, the prelates who have not had this training. He
should at least be of this level. This emerges rather more clearly in practice,

89. 1 Pet. 2:13.
90. There are few more explicit expressions of Wessels's thinking than the current
pages (/758-59/). Initially, he applies 1 Pet. 2:13 simply to the upper ranks of the ecclesiastical hierarchy: they are to proclaim the truth of the gospel and to give guidance,
in the form of both *praecepta* and *exempla*. The latter comprises giving examples, signs,
but also explanations. Wessel summarizes the entire complex of *praecepta* and *exempla*
under the term "law" (*lex*). The typesetter of the early printed edition has proceeded
with the utmost care, fully in the spirit of the author: he consistently sets "law" (*lex*)
in lower case, and gives "gospel" a capital letter. The argument tends towards the
glorification of the gospel, culminating in Augustine's dictum from his criticism of
the Manichean manifesto, the *Epistula fundamenti*. The gospel contains the truth—or
truths (as is also said)—but no one can comprehend this truth. One can only hope to
"draw near" to it (*incedere*; /748/).
91. I.e., Jesus Christ.

since anyone who is better and more clearly informed about theological truth will not, in matters of faith, easily follow what is claimed by someone who is less well informed. When it comes to belief, we are all subject first and foremost to the gospel, so that we should not believe an angel of heaven who teaches otherwise, or even St. Paul himself, as his epistle says.[92]

The church has made various changes over the years to the form of the liturgy—think, for example, of the time, place, and form of the breaking of bread—because as in successive and bygone times the purpose became different, the result became different too. It was not that it [the church] changed the sign of the Lord's Supper, for this had always remained unchanged, but it adapted the original celebration in its liturgy.[93] For the same reason, the church also changed some of the commands of the law. But it did not dare to change the gospel.[94] Where, in imitation and obedience, it believed things were suitable for change, and did then change them, it did so precisely because of the unchangeable truth of the gospel. For the gospel is the light for all questions of obedience and change. For this reason, for whoever truly knows the gospel, it has such force—so compelling is the gospel—that no multitude, no /759/ high authority can move the person who knows this not to believe. For after all, it is because of God that we believe the gospel, and because of the gospel that we believe the church and the pope; it is not that we believe the gospel because of the church.

This is why what Augustine says about the gospel and the church is a saying about the origins of faith. It does not express a comparison or a preference. For the Lord Jesus said to his apostles: "Proclaim" the gospel "to the whole of creation, teaching them to obey everything that I have commanded you."[95] You should only listen, then, to those who have been sent; they have not been sent unless they bring the gospel; and they are not evangelizing unless they preach in accordance with the gospel.[96] A single person who contradicts the entire multitude about the gospel is more likely to be mistaken than the

92. Cf. Gal. 1:8. For the office of the *doctor theologiae* as mentioned in this passage, see G. H. M. Posthumus Meyjes, *Quasi stellae fulgebunt. Plaats en functie van de theologische doctor in de middeleeuwse maatschappij en kerk* (Leiden, 1979).

93. For the changing form of the celebration of the Lord's Supper, see J. A. Jungmann, S. J., *The Mass of the Roman Rite: Its Origin and Development (Missarum Sollemnia)*, trans. F. A. Brunner, rev. Ch. K. Riepe (New York, etc., 1959), part 1, *The Form of the Mass through the Centuries*, par. 1–11, 1–91. It is impossible to deduce from the context exactly what changes Wessel is alluding to here.

94. Wessel's antithetical thinking comes to the fore again here in the relationship between the gospel and the law. Cf. n. 90.

95. Combination of Mark 16:15 and Matt. 28:20. Wessel Gansfort ultimately gives a quotation from the Gospel to support his interpretation of Augustine's well-known dictum. For his interpretation, see above, chapter 2, section 1.

96. Cf. Rom. 10:15.

whole church community of learned men, so for this reason everyone, without exception, should always suspect himself and beware of erring. But at the same time, knowing that it is not impossible for many learned people to be in error, he should, first of all, embrace the shining truth of the gospel. For that reason, secondly, he should continue diligently and carefully to seek the truth and the right understanding of the gospel. Thirdly, he should study the arguments of his opponents and should lend strong support to those that, in his opinion, are closest to the gospel.

How should we understand Christ's words about the scribes and Pharisees?

Many of those in authority in the church draw false and erroneous conclusions from the words of our Lord Jesus: "The scribes and the Pharisees sit on Moses's seat; therefore, do whatever they teach you and follow it."[97] For they believe that, on the basis of these words, the authentic power is bestowed on them to oblige those who hear them to observe and do what they say. But others, too, are mistaken about the implications of these words. They tend toward this interpretation because of the very broad scope of the formulation "do whatever they teach you and follow it."[98] But it is quite easy to bring these people to a proper understanding. For it is easy to see that one should not observe and act on all of their words. The words with which they entrap, with which they openly, deliberately, and persistently fashion perfidious lies—these are not to be observed or obeyed. And the blasphemies of the scribes and Pharisees are also not to be observed or carried out: if they say, for example, that the Lord Jesus "casts out demons by Beelzebul, the ruler of the demons,"[99] or "Whoever swears by the sanctuary is bound by nothing, but whoever swears by the gold of the sanctuary is bound by the oath."[100]

Since Jesus calls people of this kind blind men and fools /760/, why should we ignore this and follow foolish and ignorant leaders? Perhaps one might say, when the Lord Jesus spoke these words, he no longer remembered what he had said before; or when he made the earlier statement, he did not foresee what he would say later. For elsewhere he says: "Beware of the yeast of the Pharisees." And he explains this immediately: "that is, their hypocrisy."[101] He who commands us to observe and do everything they say—that same Lord commands us to beware of the yeast of their doctrine. Therefore, anyone who listens to the scribes and the Pharisees should be as innocent as the dove in

---

97. Matt. 23:2–3. Cf. /756/ above.
98. Matt. 23:3.
99. Luke 11:15.
100. Matt. 23:16–17.
101. Luke 12:1.

seeking out only the good grain.[102] But above all, he should be prudent and wise, that is, well equipped with wise astuteness, to know how to test everything in the words of the scribes and the Pharisees and to hold fast only to what is good in them.[103] The faithful listeners should be equipped with this power of discernment.[104] For scribes and Pharisees do not have the power to command, as the high priest, and those ordained under him, had. For after all, they [the scribes and the Pharisees] were not seated in the seat of a judge or a ruler, but a teaching chair, like the teachers and preachers of today.

Now the first of the errors mentioned above, which is not so widespread, entails rather more problems, since it concerns the governing power accorded to those in authority in the church.[105] But for those who can judge discerningly [it is clear] that for the people the same yardstick must be used in following the commands of prelates as when it comes to hearing the teaching of corrupt leaders. The commands of prelates and teachers must be observed and carried out as the evangelist indicates,[106] that is, as long as those who sit on Moses's seat actually speak in harmony with Moses. And if they teach something else, or something which is at variance with Moses's teaching, this is not in the slightest binding on the faithful, in the face of the law of perfect freedom.[107]

We are the servants of God, not of the Pope. And of course we would be forced to serve him, if we were obliged to obey him unconditionally. But it is said: "Worship the Lord your God, and serve only him."[108]

The blindness and foolishness of scribes and Pharisees

"And whoever swears by the sanctuary, swears by it and by the one who dwells in it; and whoever swears by heaven, swears by the throne of God and by the one who is seated upon it" (Matt. 23 [:21–22]). Whoever swears by something

102. Cf. Matt. 10:16.
103. Cf. 1 Thess. 5:21.
104. Cf. 1 Cor. 12:10.
105. The syntax in the Latin text is very complex and far from correct. However, the author's meaning is clear. He is alluding to the well-known distinction between the power of ordination (*potestas ordinis*) and the power of jurisdiction (*potestas iurisdictionis*), which reside in the ordained officeholder. Gerson's discussion about authority in the church is characterized by these two terms (*De potestate ecclesiastica*, in *Oeuvres Complètes*, no. 282, pp. 212ss.). Distinction follows distinction, as the discussion elaborates mainly on the question of power of jurisdiction. Wessel Gansfort approaches the matter more straightforwardly, and simply tests the exercise of authority in the church against a quotation from the Scriptures (Matt. 23:2–3). The misunderstanding that he picks up on (in the circles of his audience?) is the view that this statement applies only to the doctors of the church (*doctores*) and not to the governing ranks (prelates and *pastores*).
106. Cf. Matt. 23:2–3. The Latin text reads "Paulus."
107. Cf. Jas. 1:25 (the perfect law, the law of liberty).
108. Matt. 4:10.

created by his God, actually swears by his Creator. But if those foolish and blind scribes and Pharisees state or proclaim the contrary, must we then listen to them because of the words quoted above [Matt. 23:3], /761/ against the true and only master? Of course not. Unless what they teach is in accordance with him, and their teaching leads us to him. For surely nobody follows a blind and stupid leader unless he himself is blind? For this reason, the Lord Jesus is not referring only to the Pharisees, the leaders of the foolish and blind, but also to the people themselves who are led by them. For he says "foolish and blind guides of the blind."[109] Anyone who follows a blind and foolish guide is indeed blind and foolish. And when they wanted to lay their hands on the Lord, the crowd was praised. They [the scribes and Pharisees] were afraid of their stones. They did not dare to give an answer to the questions about the baptism of John.[110] The fear of being stoned made them cautious, but even then this same crowd did not deflect them from their insane plans on the following day of preparation [before the Sabbath]. For this reason, the crowd is rightfully censured by Augustine, since it thus became complicit in the murder of Christ.[111]

After the Lord Jesus has threatened the scribes and the Pharisees with seven woes,[112] he addresses, by the name Jerusalem, all those who confess doctrine and exercise pastoral care and yet do not practice even a vestige of truth or righteousness. For he says: "Jerusalem, Jerusalem, the city that kills the prophets and stones those who are sent to it." The fact that he is referring only to them is clear from the context, since he adds: "How often have I desired to gather your children together as a hen gathers her brood under her wings, and you were not willing!"[113]

Here one can clearly discern three groups: Jerusalem, children of Jerusalem, and the Lord Jesus, who wishes to gather these children like a brooding hen. The second group are the children of Jerusalem who should be gathered under the hen's wings. The third category is formed by those who do not wish to be gathered under the hen's wings: those who lead people astray, blind and foolish pastors and teachers. And here I ask: if the *doctores* and *pastores* of the third category obstruct and contradict, with their machinations, the hen who wishes to gather them in, to whom should the hen's chicks lis-

109. Combination of Matt. 15:14 and Matt. 23:16–17.
110. Cf. Luke 20:1–8.
111. I have not been able to find the passage in question in Augustine's works. It is probably taken from a pseudo-Augustininian writing (suggestion of Dr. De Meijer, Eindhoven). Augustine even more vehemently accuses the Jews of complicity in the murder of Christ in his *Tractatus in Psalmum LXIII* [64], 1–4; CChr 39:807–10: *et uos, o Iudaei, occidistis* (810).
112. Cf. Matt. 23:13–36.
113. Matt. 23:37.

ten? Even if the Lord Jesus does say, "Do whatever they teach you to do and follow it,"[114] the chicks—unless they are blind and foolish—will surely take refuge under the wings of the hen as soon as the hireling pastor barks at the true Pastor. But why did the Lord Jesus address this matter in such breadth? Surely purely so that we should focus our attention on comparing scriptural passages that concur with one another and explain one another? Otherwise we would not penetrate so deeply into what is written as does the wisdom that comes from careful study. Thus exercising wisdom and truth is its own reward. /762/

What does Christ mean in saying that we should not listen to preachers and pastors?

We should pay close attention to what our Lord Jesus Christ means when, in the last address of the whole Gospel, Matthew 23, he draws the conclusion that we should not listen to teachers, preachers, and pastors when they teach, preach, and feed their flocks at odds with their duty and skills. For these are hypocrites and vain creatures, who "do all their deeds to be seen by others."[115]

They are ambitious: they seek out the best seats at banquets and the places of honor in the synagogue. They are vain creatures, who take pleasure in vain things and want to be greeted in the marketplaces and addressed as "rabbi." They are avaricious people who devour widows' houses.[116] They are play actors, if they get the chance, under the guise of praying long prayers.[117] They are corrupt and pestilent, because though they are entrusted with authority over the kingdom, they themselves do not put their service of God into practice. And they prevent others who wish to exercise this faithfully. This is why the Lord Jesus is reproaching them when he says, "But woe to you, scribes and Pharisees, hypocrites! For you lock people out of the kingdom of heaven. For you do not go in yourselves, and when others are going in, you stop them,"[118] They are pseudoteachers, for they teach the people lies instead of the truth of saving faith. They teach, for example, that an oath by the temple or altar is not binding, whereas an oath made by the gift offered up is.[119] They are perverse, for they strain out a gnat from their cup, but swallow a camel. They ignore the weightier matters of the law, but these perverse people are strict when it comes to minor matters.[120] The commands of men they carry out with strict precision, but what God wills they trample underfoot; for they

---

114. Matt. 23:3.
115. Matt. 23:5. For the following section, cf. Matt. 23:6–7.
116. Mark 12:40.
117. Matt. 23:14.
118. Matt. 23:13.
119. Cf. Matt. 23:18.
120. Cf. Matt. 23:23–24.

are not willing to gather their children together under the wings of the hen, warm and safe.[121]

Since they are like this, which of the two should their subjects, for whom the kingdom of heaven is at hand, then follow? Those who do not wish to enter themselves, and try to prevent others who do wish to do so?[122] Or him who is always quick to be merciful throughout our entire lives and who wishes to gather them together under his wings?[123] In this situation, they must of course listen to the mother hen, not to those false, vain, ostentatious, ambitious, avaricious, and perverse people, those pseudoteachers, worthless preachers, foolish and blind prelates, the blind leading the blind.[124]

Nevertheless, the believers are obliged to maintain them in their position—to the extent that they [the believers] are obliged to do and observe what they have said rightly and sanely. But if they speak or teach wickedly, the believers should not obey them, unless they choose to be blind among the blind, excluded from under the wings of the hen[125] /763/ and from the kingdom of heaven, corrupt and infected by those who spread ruin. For how could these people not sow death and destruction, these people whom Jesus calls "snakes" and the "brood of vipers"?[126]

For after all, the apostle says explicitly, "Bad company ruins good morals."[127] And could there be any talk more depraved than that of corrupt teachers, pastors, priests, or prelates? Their words are like a spreading cancer[128]—and not only their words, but also the bad example they give.

All evil is prone to imitation. But if anyone "put a stumbling-block before any of these little ones," whether he be the pope or any other pastor—that is, by deflecting them from the right path, from their progress along the way of the Lord, through perverse doctrines, neglect of his ministry, or corrupt example—it would be better for him if a great millstone were fastened around his neck and he were drowned in the depth of the sea.[129] This would be better than for him to lead people into ruin and destruction.

Each and every prelate who gives simple people occasion to sin is an Antichrist

Everyone, no matter how high his authority or dignity, is an antichrist if he gives simple people occasion to sin and—against the will of Christ—holds

121. Cf. Matt. 23:37.
122. Cf. Matt. 23:13.
123. Cf. Matt. 23:37.
124. Cf. Matt. 15:14.
125. Cf. Matt. 23:37.
126. Cf. Matt. 23:33.
127. 1 Cor. 15:33.
128. Cf. 2 Tim. 2:17.
129. Cf. Matt. 18:6.

them back from the pure paths that lead to truth and life.[130] For every such person is trying, against Christ's will, to bring about the ruin of those for whom Christ poured out his blood.[131] Plunging into ruin those whom Christ endeavored to save with his death—what is that other than resisting Christ? Christ wishes to save by his obedience;[132] but many prelates, through their disobedience to the commandments and their bad example, do not care about the stumbling block they form to all the points that the Lord Jesus summarizes for the people in Matthew 23. If this is true—and that is what I believe, unless I am informed better—these simple faithful must be advised by a good person and admonished not to stumble into sin. But if these people are not informed about all the individual abuses and the ruinous, bad examples of the prelates and warned against them, they will scarcely be able to avoid them.

If we explain these matters in this way, we will soon stir up these hypocritical, ostentatious, ambitious, vain, licentious, avaricious prelates, not only against ourselves, but also against the people in their charge. But the Lord Jesus forbade passive inducements to sin,[133] and publicly denounced the infamies of all these troublemakers. Not only did he uncover the infamies of the troublemakers, but he also called down eternal woe /764/ on them.[134]

But he who wishes to follow the example of the Lord Jesus should know that when he preached this he was already prepared to bear the cross. If you do not wish to follow that example, you must simply resign yourself to the fact that stumbling blocks can spring up unhindered all over the place. For you always have to make sure that the remedy is not worse than the disease.[135] These are dangerous times.[136] And why are they dangerous? Surely

130. Wessel gives a broad and "inclusive" definition of the term "antichrist," based on a literal interpretation of the word: anti-Christ refers to anyone who plunges others into ruin, against the wishes of Christ (cf. 1 John 2:18-22 and 4:3; 2 John 7). In this way, he indirectly relativizes the views of the Cathars, Waldensians, and Wycliffites, according to whom the pope was the antichrist. But this definition does allow him to include prelates of the church under the label of antichrist.

131. Cf. Matt. 26:28, Mark 14:24, and Luke 22:20.

132. Cf. Rom. 5:19 and Heb. 5:8–9.

133. Being a stumbling block, an occasion or inducement to sin, is called "passive" if a given form of behavior is not expressly intended to induce another person to sin, but this is in fact what occurs. This is what prompts Christ to pronounce his sevenfold "Woe to you." In the penultimate paragraph of this section, Wessel illustrates clearly that this passive inducement is twofold: that of the simple of heart (*pusillorum*) and that of the Pharisees (*pharisaicum*).

134. Cf. Matt. 23:13–36.

135. The well-known truism that the remedy may be worse than the disease it seeks to cure. Wessel views Christ's outspoken stance against the scribes and the Pharisees as a sign of his willingness to die a violent death. The same fate may well befall anyone who follows his example.

136. Cf. 2 Tim. 3:1.

it is because everywhere the prelates of the church are corrupt. And though the Lord Jesus spoke these words to the scribes and the Pharisees, it was not for their sake. For the kingdom of heaven was soon to be withdrawn from them anyway. No, what he preached related to times that were then far off. It was for our sake that this was written down.[137] We are threatened by the same danger at the hand of our pastors, preachers, and teachers, if they are not saved. For at the end of chapter 24, the Lord Jesus expressly refers to two types of servants that will be put in charge of his household.[138] Some of them he calls good and faithful, and these feed the family at the right time; the other servants are useless. When their master is away, they are seized by foolish and evil notions. They set to reveling and getting drunk, behave arrogantly, and exercise tyranny over their fellow servants. Anyone who is corrupted by their example and falls into the pit with them cannot excuse himself due to ignorance, blindness, or foolishness. Anyone who is induced to sin due to blindness or foolishness is himself blind and foolish, since through his own blindness he wholeheartedly participates in the excesses of those servants and follows them in their excesses. But anyone who is led into sin by healthy teachings and a good example, and ends up the worse for it, should not be reckoned among the simple-hearted, but rather among the scribes and the Pharisees;[139] for he has spurned Wisdom's advice. He has stoned and killed the prophets and Wisdom will rejoice and laugh at his downfall.[140]

Thus passive inducement[141] to sin is twofold: on the one hand there is inducing the simple-hearted to sin, and on the other hand inducing the Pharisees to sin. The Lord Jesus says of the latter that it is better for them to be induced to sin than for the truth to be suppressed. The simple-hearted are induced into sin because of evil, the Pharisees because of good.

It may happen that somebody has leadership powers bestowed on him, but not wisdom. The authority he exercises has no dignity; it consists merely of power. But because no power is given to operate at variance with wisdom and truth, power should never be bestowed on leaders who are blind. For if someone follows a blind leader and falls into a pit because of that blindness, his fall is not made any the less by the leader's authority. /765/

To what extent are subordinates obliged to obey their prelates and superiors?

It is worth considering to what extent a subordinate is obliged to obey those in authority in the church, and a lower-ranking person his superiors. For this is

137. Cf. Rom. 15:4.
138. Cf. Matt. 24:45.
139. Cf. Matt. 23:37.
140. Cf. Prov. 1:26.
141. See n. 133 above.

not an obligation that stems from someone's condition in life,[142] which would
be an absolute obligation. Rather it is an obligation founded on an agreement
with a prelate.[143] For this superior is not the master over his subordinates, even
if these subordinates call him "Lord" and the superiors sometimes behave in
this way for good reasons. For if those in authority in the church do not keep
to the rules in accordance with the obligations set out in the agreement, the
subordinates will also not be obliged to fulfill all their obligations. The obligations apply to the subordinates in the same measure as the authorities fulfill
their obligations. If, then, someone in authority in the church simply sets aside
that law, the subordinate too is no longer bound by any obligation. For this
obligation must be voluntary and wholehearted. For this reason, one should
not enter into such an obligation without due deliberation. In this deliberation, he will take into account the motives and the fruits of the agreement.
If the motives and fruits are such that they could convince the deliberator
before the contract is entered into, they can equally dissolve the obligation on
the same grounds if one of the parties defaults. For this reason, it is virtually
in the nature of this obligation that the subordinates should elect their own
superior. For they will choose someone whom they believe will best protect
their own interests and the motivations for their choice.

The mendicant orders seem to go about this election process with the greatest care. Every year they renew their choice for their own community, even if
they do not elect a new superior each year.[144] But if there was one to whom

142. See Niermeyer *Mediae* (n. 45), 313, under *condicio/conditio*.
143. Cf. /752/ above. In contrast to the established hierarchical structures of the
church of his day, Wessel Gansfort's view of obedience to the ecclesiastical authorities—as an obligation entered into "freely and from the heart"—fully deserves to be
termed revolutionary. The hierarchical structure of the church, forcefully reinforced
by the writings of Pseudo-Dionysius (see /754/ above) is repeatedly underpinned
legally in the CIC. See, for example, the rubric *De maioritate et obedientia* and perhaps
the best-known document of the history of the late medieval church: the bull *Unam
sanctam* of Pope Boniface VIII (d. 1303). See CIC *Extravagantes Communes*, Lib. I, Tit.
VIII. This pope, too, cites Pseudo-Dionysius for the steplike hierarchical structure of
authority in the church: "For according to the blessed Dionysius it is a divine law that
the lower forms of authority are related back to the highest authority via the interme-
diate forms" (*Infima per media in suprema reduci*). It seems to me that Wessel breaks
through this hierarchical structure of authority in the church. Cf. Johan Huizinga,
Waning (n. 14), 56–66: "The Hierarchic Conception of Society."
144. The emergence of the mendicant orders can be viewed as an attempt to
breathe new life into the church in a radical, evangelical sense. The Franciscans and
Dominicans were among these communities from the outset, in the thirteenth century. See DThC VIA, pp. 809–63 (*Frères Mineurs*), and pp. 863–924 (*Frères Prêcheurs*).
Later—in Wessel Gansfort's day—the Carmelites and the Augustinian Friars were
also numbered among the mendicants. Electing their own superior for a fixed, limited,
period—the general of the Franciscans, for example, was appointed for a maximum of
six years—played a significant role in the rules of the mendicant orders.

they could not safely entrust themselves, they would be able to choose a better one in his place. For if he were to change for the worse as circumstances changed, it would be better for both parties if they were to part company.

For whatever else one may dream up about the bond between the bishop and the church, alluding to the matrimonial bond between the bride and the bridegroom,[145] this is not an unbreakable bond [with a church], but an oath of due faith; otherwise a certificate of divorce[146] would not be possible under any circumstances. For really the bishop is not the bridegroom; rather he should be the friend of the bridegroom,[147] although he very often is not. Bishops should always be removed from their position if they are unworthy to lead. And they are always unworthy if their leadership does not bear fruit. But they are maintained, mainly because people fear even greater problems, just as is the case with the prostitutes in our cities.

A similar situation should hold for kings. In that way, in every well-instituted state the highest authority would be restrained from abuse of power by limiting either his period of office or his authority—by appointing him by the year, for example, or by a consensus in an electoral college.[148] Surely is not freedom of choice what an election signifies?[149] /766/ For one should

145. The presentation of the crosier and ring on the consecration of a bishop was already an established tradition in France by 835 (see the correspondence of Pope Nicholas I; MSL 124, p. 874). In the explication of these rituals, the crosier is interpreted as a symbol for spiritual power, the ring as a symbol for the mystical union between the bishop and the church. In other words, there is a matrimonial bond between the two.

146. Cf. Matt. 5:31 and 19:7. What Wessel means here is that the union between a bishop and his church is a *union of faith*. This remains in force, even if the prelate takes up a different office. "Church," then, must here mean diocese, since otherwise the line of argument would not make sense.

147. Cf. John 3:29.

148. Here Wessel turns his attention to the functioning of secular authority. It is not clear whether he has a particular city in mind with his criticisms (Groningen perhaps?). What is clear, though, is that his critical wishes bear a relation to the apparently democratic changes that occurred in the governance of late-medieval cities. The free city of Strasbourg in the Holy Roman Empire serves as a good example of this: in this period the guilds acquired greater political influence, and the city council, elected and assisted by various council colleges, was headed by four *Stettmeister* (elected for just one year), and the *Ammeister*, who was also elected annually. In times of crisis, the council of the guilds played an important role. See *Histoire de Strasbourg*, Sous la direction de Georges Livet et Francis Rapp (1987), 115–16 ("Des gouvernants experimentés et disponibles"). In Groningen, four members of the merchant guild served as mayor from the fourteenth century. See LvM, 4:1724–25 (J. C. Visser).

149. In the church, bishops were traditionally chosen by the clergy and the people. Wessel also advocates this. See /765/ above. This freedom in electing ecclesiastical leaders is also specified in canon law, for example in the stipulation, "The choice must be arrived at with the freedom of the electorate. Any custom which is at variance with this is invalid" (CIC *Decr. Greg.* Lib. I, Tit. VI, C. 14).

obey the best person, and an election should point to him. If an election fails to do so, one should not obey it. For this reason men of substance distance themselves from these persons, as long as they can do so honorably and with good conscience. They seek exemptions that excuse them.[150] And common law provides them with an abundance of them.

On this basis, not only should we not obey kings in the evil that they advocate, but they may justly be deposed from their rule, unless there is reason to fear that repairing the damage done would give rise to even worse damage.[151] For it is generally agreed that it is a waste of time and expense, if the damage sustained is repaired with a worse wound.

We are under a greater obligation to agree with wise people than with the pope

If a wise person's opinion differs from that of the pope, you would be better to be in line with and follow the wise person than the pope. For the pope cannot absolve an excommunication pronounced by a wise person. Remember that saying: "Let anyone be accursed who has no love for the Lord Jesus."[152] No pope can undo these words or absolve those who are bound by them. For to the extent that anyone does not love God, he is cut off from God and banned from communion with him. Even if he is in a state of salvation and grace, he can have no part in that marital union of embraces and kisses that the loving [soul] experiences. For there is a great deal of difference between him who desires, him who esteems, and him who loves.[153] Therefore, he who fears God will be excluded from the class of those who desire him; he who desires from the class of those who esteem him; and those who esteem will be excluded from that sublime and exalted class of those who love him.

What must we do if the pope and a wise man contradict one another?

In the case of hostility or contradiction between the pope and a wise man, the pope is obliged to listen to the wise man and follow him. But it is not only the pope who is thus obliged: the wise man himself, in those matters in which

150. It remains unclear what exemptions Wessel is alluding to here, and what existing law they apply to.

151. This type of radical pronouncement is typical of Wessel's position as regards the right to resist *in causa religionis*. See chap. 3, n. 58.

152. Cf. 1 Cor. 16:22.

153. Cf. Gerson, *De mystica theologia*, ed. André Combes (Lugano [1958]), 216. Gerson too describes the highest step of loving God as *amplexus sponsi* and *oscula castissima*. The distinction between *diligere* and *amare* fits within the terminology of the *Devotio moderna*, in which the terms, which characterize the gradual ascent to God, are weighed up and pondered, illuminated, and examined. The primary meaning of *di-ligere* is "to take apart, separate, and select on the basis of quality," which leads to the meaning "to esteem, respect." This is the penultimate step in the ascent to God.

he is truly wise—that is, the matters in which the word of true wisdom has been confided in him according to the immaculate law of the Lord—must not deviate in any way from his opinion or follow the authority of the pope. But the whole community of the faithful, who recognize the rightness of the wise man's words, must similarly confirm their approval of the wise man.

This is precisely what occurred recently at the Council of Constance, when the faithful did not agree with Pope John XXII [= XXIII] and affirmed their approval of Jean Gerson.[154] And if Pope Eugene and Bernard of Clairvaux were to contradict one another and disagree today, who would not side with Bernard rather than with Eugene? Eugene teaches this by his own example, /767/ since he wholeheartedly accepted the large number of strict admonitions and reproofs in [Bernard's] *De consideratione*.[155] It is the task of the theologian, then—if he practices his art properly—to define the extent to which the pope's commands are incumbent on us. "Who is he, that we may praise him?"[156] Therefore the consensus of wise people will bind the church together in unity more than does the leadership of the prelates. For the consensus of wise people is forcefully directed by God. This is frequently not the case with the regime of the prelates. For when the blind lead the blind, they often abandon them or allow them to stray.[157]

The reigning pope is often a pseudoapostle, and the prelate in office a false pastor

A prelate properly in office is one who sits on St Peter's seat by legitimate title. This title is viewed as legitimate if it is based on a canonically established election or on appointment by a higher official.[158] It follows from this that the reigning pope is often a pseudoapostle, the prelate in office a false shepherd, and the de facto head of the church a false bishop.[159] For this reason, the

154. Pope John XXIII was deposed at the Council of Constance, partly through the offices of Jean Gerson. See above, /748/, n. 31.

155. Pope Eugene III (1145–53) was a pupil of Bernard of Clairvaux (d. 1153). Bernard wrote his *De consideratione* (1149–52) at the pope's request. Wessel rates Francis of Assisi (1181–1226) more highly than the mighty Pope Honorius III (1216–27), the successor to Innocent III. See /769/ below.

156. Sir. 31:9.

157. Cf. Matt. 15:14.

158. The election of a pope was first established under canon law at the Lateran Council of 1059. Here the privilege of electing a new pope was reserved for cardinals. Since 1378, as a rule only cardinals have been eligible to become pope. Cf. Fuhrmann, *Einladung ins Mittelalter*, 135–50.

159. A peculiar syllogism, which, in its complete lack of logic, must be taken as sarcastic. By this reasoning, being correctly appointed in accordance with the tenets of canon law is no guarantee—in Wessel Gansfort's opinion—that the holder of the office is a true pastor. But perhaps Wessel simply means to say that there are prelates who lack either form of appointment. I am very grateful to Prof. Christoph Burger (Vrie Universiteit Amsterdam) for this suggestion and several others.

people must frequently resign themselves to pseudoapostles and pseudoevan-gelists, pseudobishops and pseudopastors. For to do otherwise might result in an even worse tear.[160]

If a pope does not edify, he is engaged only in dangerous endeavors

The pope must be a faithful and wise slave,[161] like a skilled and dedicated phy-sician for a person who is ill. Just as an unskilled or negligent physician may be nothing but a danger to a person who is ill, the same also holds for the highest pontiff: if he does not carry out everything that he does reliably, wisely, and with integrity—or goes against these values—all he does is nothing. For he was appointed so that he might build.[162] If he does not build, he does nothing. If someone is appointed to lead and does not carry out this mission faithfully, he effectively scatters [his flock]. Under an inferior and unreliable hireling pastor the flock will perish. With his drunken and sleepy head, no sane mem-ber of the flock will trust him when he promises safety and salvation.

How completely differently did the Lord Jesus entrust the keys of the kingdom of heaven to St. Peter and the apostles—very differently from our prelates.[163] The faithful and wise slave, whom his master has put in charge over his household, gives them a measure of wheat at the proper time, that is, the best sort of food.[164] He is solicitous to serve God in a multitude of ways: in vigilant care, in prayer, by his good example in leading the way. He is there for his people, as a wise and worthy leader should be there to help his peo-ple. But in our own prelates we see negligence, lasciviousness, carelessness, pomp, self-importance. They are censorious and strict, since they are intent on observing their mandates as a cover for retaining their power. /768/

I do not believe, therefore, that this has anything to do with the keys to the kingdom of heaven. Rather this is the key of the Pharisees, with which they cannot go into the kingdom themselves[165]—for one cannot go in this way—and with which they stop others from going in. These others are corrupted

---

160. Cf. Matt. 9:16.
161. Cf. Matt. 24:45.
162. Cf. 2 Cor. 10:8: "our authority, which the Lord gave for building you up and not for tearing you down." The concept of constructiveness/edification is key in Wes-sel's argument about authority in the church. This approach puts him in the company of Jean Gerson. See Gerson's *De potestate ecclesiastica*, in *Oeuvres Complètes*, no. 282, pp. 211, 225, 232, and 239.
163. Cf. Matt. 16:13–20, esp. v. 19, and Matt. 18:18. Wessel's wording—"to Peter and the apostles"—is striking. This is possibly an echo of Gerson, who repeatedly argues, also with reference to Augustine, that the keys of the kingdom of heaven were entrusted to the whole body of the apostles (*unitas*). See Gerson, op. cit., 217 and 232.
164. Cf. Matt. 24:45.
165. Cf. Matt. 23:13.

and obstructed by their bad example, no matter how much they fight for the key to power—and fight they certainly do!

For in fact the key, a much greater and truer one, is piety.[166] Without this key, the key of power is powerless. Wherever this key [of piety] has been used, the key of power has always been found to be joined to it. Peter and Paul would never have opened the door of the kingdom of heaven to the Gentiles for these machinations [of the prelates]. If they had spoken on the basis of their own wisdom, application, and example, they would never have liberated the Gentiles from their yoke of slavery and corruption.

This is clear from their followers.[167] Just as these followers are allied to them, their norms and values are in line with theirs. For in all cathedral, collegiate churches, which have the fattest incomes, it is always the closest associates of the pope and the cardinals who hold the keys to the coffers. And how edifying is *their* lifestyle? Is it perhaps different from where they come from, where they were appointed? Nobody would have opened the door to a kingdom in the manner in which the cardinals insult the apostles and their disciples,[168] not in Jerusalem under the Roman governor and high priests, not in Antioch, and not in Rome. There heavier weapons were needed, against the will of Nero and the will of the Senate. I am talking about the door to the kingdom of heaven. For perhaps he could have opened the door to his *own* kingdom in this way. But once love had been poured into their hearts by the Holy Spirit,[169] and they were strengthened by love and inspired by love and fortitude to proclaim the gospel and to suffer for the salvation of the believers, then the Lord cooperated with them[170] to throw open the door of salvation and of his kingdom to all believers. It was not Peter who gave them faith within. He merely sowed the word of the gospel from the outside. There is no greater grace, wisdom, and justice for anyone than is found in this handwritten or printed book.[171]

166. Together with "edification" (*aedificatio*, οἰκοδομή), this is the other key term for Wessel's perspective on ecclesiastical authority: piety (*pietas*: "Without this key all power is powerless").

167. This and the following sentence are again intended ironically.

168. The Latin text is anything but clear and unambiguous here. What Wessel wishes to say is that the gospel would never have taken root if the preachers of the early church had gone about their work in the same way as the church leaders of his own day.

169. Cf. Rom. 5:5.

170. Allusion to Mark 16:20.

171. Here too the Latin text is not entirely clear. Wessel emphasizes that even someone who proclaims the gospel cannot automatically implant faith. He sees a certain opposition between the "inner" and the "outer" word. In my translation I interpret the passage in a way that possibly makes sense.

Explanation of the words of the apostle: "There is no authority except from God"

The apostle states that "there is no authority except from God, and those authorities that exist have been instituted by God. Therefore whoever resists authority resists what God has appointed."[172] These words should not be read or understood superficially or perfunctorily. Those in authority can err both in physical and /769/ in spiritual matters. They can err greatly and thus form a stumbling block to their subjects on their way to God, plunging those who obey them into mortal error.

This can be seen clearly in the history of the Roman emperors who persecuted the Christians for their faith and their piety. Laurence and Vincent resisted them forcefully and steadfastly.[173] Even if the people, inflamed by piety, had taken up arms against those raging emperors and had overcome their madness in this way, I do not believe they would have committed a mortal sin through this resistance. For Augustine even links the murder of our Lord with the tacit consent of the crowd, in that they did not put up any resistance to the pressure of their leaders.[174] And Ambrose believes, along with Gregory, that in society there are hidden scruples against crime that disappear as soon as it manifests itself.[175]

The apostle's words about authority should be understood, as he himself puts it slightly differently elsewhere, to mean there is no authority except insofar as it is constructive.[176] For so long as authority is constructive, it comes from God; if it is not constructive, the person who is constructive through resistance has received the power to resist from God.[177] So, being constructive is authority that comes from God, and he who is the most constructive has the most authority. This means that Paul has more authority than Peter, Bernard more than Innocent or Eugene, and Francis more than Honorius.[178]

Subjects have the right to admonish their prelates: "And say to Archippus, 'See that you complete the task that you have received in the Lord.'"[179] Yes,

172. Rom. 13:1–2.
173. Laurence, a deacon in Rome under the emperor Valerian, was martyred in 258. Vincent was a legendary deacon and martyr from Agen (Aquitaine). The date of his death is not known.
174. See n. 111.
175. I have not been able to trace this statement in the works of either Ambrose or Gregory.
176. Cf. 2 Cor. 10:8.
177. It would be impossible to find a stronger formulation of the right to resist, and on the basis of Rom. 13, too! The echoes of this dictum can still be heard in Reformation Strasbourg. See below, chap. 3, n. 58.
178. See n. 55 above.
179. Col. 4:17.

they are even ordered to distance themselves from any brother who lives rest-lessly and inordinately.[180] Thus this holds all the more for a corrupt prelate.

A corrupt clergy is most destructive for the church

Nobody destroys the church more than a corrupt clergy. All Christians must resist those who destroy the church. And there are no exceptions to this. Think, for example, of people without any education, in accordance with the saying "Just as pious, uneducated people build up the church of God by a wor-thy life, they also damage it if they do not resist those who destroy it."[181]

The dissoluteness of prelates and princes has its origin in the worthlessness and folly of the people

All error, all licentiousness, all the dissoluteness of prelates, princes, and kings have their origin in the evil, worthlessness, and folly of the people. This is amply demonstrated by excellent, large cities—wherever they are—in which the licentiousness of the rulers is minor. It is even more evident from particu-larly well-governed /770/ monasteries run by the best religious. There, a prel-ate will beware of allowing himself to deviate from the straight and narrow. And if he ever thought differently, he would not long be tolerated.

The clearest demonstration of this, however, is the story of John the Bap-tist, who accused the king of unacceptable behavior, and was not prepared to tolerate his misconduct.[182] And if the majority of the people had been as wise as he, they would not have sustained the king in his reign unless he had bet-tered his ways. For, like all rulers, these types spring forth from the sinfulness of the people.[183] That is the nest in which they originate. No wonder, then, that the viper [an evil ruler] is threatened already at its birth if the people are publicly tyrannized by the ruler both in family matters and in heavy servitude. For he has no idea of the damage that he inflicts on their piety and religious

180. Cf. 2 Thess. 3:6: "that you keep away from any brother who is living in idle-ness and not in accord with the tradition that you received from us" (*Greek English New Testament*, 26th rev. ed. [Stuttgart, 1981]).

181. I have not been able to establish the origin of this maxim. Perhaps it derives from Wessel himself.

182. Cf. Mark 6:14–29.

183. Herod Antipas was responsible for the execution of John the Baptist (Mark 6). Antipas was the youngest son of Herod the Great, whose name is associated with the murder of the innocents in Bethlehem (Matt. 2). Perhaps one should read this section as an allusion to that event. Antipas was equally the uncle of Herod Agrippa, who in turn had John's brother James put to death (Acts 12). Apparently this Herodian dynasty is the model Wessel Gansfort has in mind in condemning all the princely dynasties of his own day. But the remarkable aspect of this passage is that, just as in relation to authority within the context of the church, Wessel holds the subjects partly responsible for the abuses perpetrated.

devotion to God. Let him experience this for himself in public. Then, having experienced hardship in public, he may learn to listen and understand the message of the far greater damage he inflicts on inner values.[184]

About the dispensation given by prelates.[185] What is its basis? Why is it not necessary to apply for it? Why do people apply for it?

Even before the gospel was proclaimed, there were not only differences but also a ranking in the commandments that had to be kept. The scribes of the Jews recognized this. But the Lord Jesus himself also explains this in a saying from his own lips, when he says: The first of all the commandments is "You shall love the Lord your God with all your heart, and with all your soul," etc. This is the first commandment. And the second is like it: "You shall love your neighbor as yourself."[186] And when the scribe confessed that these commandments are greater than all sacrifices and burnt offerings, the Lord, since he saw that the man had answered wisely, assured him that he was not far from the kingdom of God.[187]

It is true that these two commandments are greater than all burnt offerings. But this order of importance has the following result: in cases where two commandments of the law clash, the greater and prior commandment always cancels out the lesser commandment. For there can be no contradiction in the law of God. Therefore perplexity can never arise in serving God.[188] This truth forms the firm foundation at the basis of all prelates' authorities to issue dispensations. Moreover, since no contradiction can exist within the law of God (and thus the servants of God can never be perplexed), this means that if it is impossible to obey two commandments, every loyal servant of God is [automatically] bound to focus directly on the greater commandment. No dispensation from the lesser commandment is necessary.

The Lord Jesus also gives an example of a clash between two commandments of the law: the commandment /771/ to honor one's parents and the

184. Cf. Isa. 28:19. I am grateful to Cornelis Augustijn for pointing out this parallel.

185. The original meaning of "dispensation" is "the balanced sharing out of communal goods between the members." From this the term came to have the meaning of "governing" or "administering." Later it was used, especially by Greek patristic authors, to designate any deviation from the normal rules of the law in cases of necessity (διοίκησις). In canon law it becomes a technical term for deviation from the law in a specific case. Cf. *Codex Iuris Canonici*, can. 80.

186. Cf. Mark 12:29–31.

187. Cf. Mark 12:33–34.

188. This refers to the impossible situation (despair, *perplexitas*) in which the believer is forced to choose in his conscience between two commandments, but believes that whichever he chooses will result in a sin. Such a situation can never arise, Wessel posits, since the more important commandment will always outweigh the other.

commandment to present offerings.[189] The former of the two is a law of nature and necessary; the latter is voluntary and an act of free will. For the commandment to support one's parents and attend to their needs is greater than any sacrifice or burnt offering, as is the commandment to stand by one's neighbor in his time of need. And this holds even if one has promised a sacrifice by oath. The fact that dispensations are sought in such situations occurs either from fear of one's own ignorance or because pressure is exerted from elsewhere.

189. Cf. Mark 7:10–12.

3

Martin Bucer and Wessel Gansfort

Exploratory Forays

The relationship between Wessel Gansfort and Martin Bucer was more complex than appears on the surface. This chapter brings together some exploratory forays into that relationship. It begins by examining Bucer's explicit citation of Wessel in his 1536 Romans commentary. The next section explores the various ways in which the influence of Wessel's texts on the Eucharist and church authority can be traced in Bucer's work. The third section identifies linguistic similarities between phrases in the writings of the usually prolix reformer and the much sharper antithetical expressions of Wessel Gansfort. The fourth and fifth sections focus on the treatise of Wessel Gansfort that Bucer cites, and the Dutch theologian's related views of creation, associated with his praise for Francis of Assisi. A concluding comment makes a further comparison of Wessel Gansfort and Martin Bucer with regard to their use of nominalism. A final note returns to Augustine's dictum, which Wessel Gansfort formulated for Bucer, reflecting that this remarkable saying not only has a history through the late Middle Ages into the Reformation, but it may have a future as well.

1. INTRODUCTION

Bucer's Commentary on Romans 8:18

Martin Bucer's interest in creation, and more particularly in how God's creation can be restored to its initial harmony, is evident even from his first publication: *Das ym selbs* (1523).[1] In effect, his first publication is a writing of reconciliation.[2]

1. Martin Bucer, *Deutsche Schriften* (BDS), ed. R. Stupperich (Gütersloh, 1960), 1:29–67.
2. M. de Kroon, *Eén van ons. Perspectief op verzoening* (Zoetermeer, 1999), 35–41.

The importance Bucer attaches to creation is developed in detail in his exegesis of Romans 8:18–23.[3] Humanity and creation are blood relations.[4] But the poison of sin[5] has eroded their former harmonious relationship. The reconciliation effected by Christ also heralds the restoration of good relations between humankind and creation.

How will this come about? Bucer devotes an extensive passage to this question in his commentary on Romans 8:18 ("I am even convinced that the suffering of the current times are as nothing beside the splendor that will be revealed to us").[6] This passage opens with the question, "When humankind attains incorruptibility and immortality, will the universe also be renewed?"[7] "For this reason," Bucer posits, "some people wonder whether plants, living creatures, and the like will also be restored." No Christian can ignore this question, he believes. For "my Redeemer will liberate all this from the servitude that leads to ruin." The reader senses clearly how personally the commentator feels concerned by these questions. "I shall ponder this matter, I shall ruminate on it again." He views all exegesis of the Scriptures as a path and a vocation to renew one's life. For himself, and for all creation, he hopes for complete happiness, that is, the restoration that will lead to resurrection. "For me it is enough that I, and all creation, will experience a happiness I cannot now even conceive of." He concludes the introductory part of this passage with a prayer of thanksgiving and exultation. The above lines probably give us a good sense of what he was like as a lecturer.[8] This personal tone pervades his entire exegesis.

Bucer Chooses Wessel Gansfort

One should not think, Bucer insists, that "creation" here refers only to humankind. This would be too narrow a definition, only lukewarm. There is a great deal more to it than mere humanity, and that is no exaggeration, no

---

3. *Metaphrases et enarrationes perpetuae epistolarum D. Pauli Apostoli . . . Tomus primus, Continens metaphrasin et enarrationem in Epistolam ad Romanos (Comm. Rom.)* (Strasbourg, 1536), 339–46.

4. "This refers to a mysterious relationship that all things have in common with human beings." Op. cit., 341b.

5. Cf. *Eén van ons* (n. 2), 38.

6. *Comm. Rom.*, 343a–346a.

7. Op. cit., 343a. For the following, see 343a–b.

8. Bucer began his exegetical studies of Paul's Epistle to the Romans in 1534. This gave rise to his *opus magnum*, the colossal commentary on this epistle. See M. Greschat, *Martin Bucer. Ein Reformator und seine Zeit* (Munich, 1990), 68 and 93–94, and B. Roussel, *Martin Bucer, lecteur de l'Epitre aux Romains* (theol. diss. [typescript], vols. 1–2, 1970), 1:14–17.

matter what Chrystostom may believe.[9] As Bucer sees it, this would go against
the Scriptures, since the promised renewal embraces the entire cosmos, "that
work of art that is the world, in all its parts. The prophets foretold this, as did
Paul in Colossians 1 and Peter in his second epistle [3:13]."

Augustine too falls short of the mark, in Bucer's estimation. Here Bucer
alludes to *De civitate Dei* [XX]16,[10] reproaching the church father for limiting
the restoration of the cosmos to the elements. Augustine never gives a thought
to other matters, understanding the new heaven and new earth prophesied by
Isaiah as "simply that."[11]

Thomas Aquinas, in his *Summa theologiae* 3, q.91, is also found wanting.
At least Thomas does apply a well-considered yardstick, which he believes he
finds in creation itself: only that which pertains to humankind, to humanity's
status of incorruptibility, will be renewed.[12] Bucer can understand this opinion to a certain extent, but he does not share it. And here, unexpectedly, he
poses a key question: "Why cannot that which is mortal and weak be granted
immortality?"[13] This is clearly an allusion to 1 Corinthians 15:54. For surely
everything is subject to God's almighty power? He can give life to a temporal
existence, but equally to eternal being.[14] He created everything from nothing,
including the heavens and the heavenly bodies. These are nothing more than
ephemerae, day flies.[15] "As that devout man Ioannes Wessel[!] so aptly put it,
nature is nothing other than the ordered will of God, just as a miracle is the
unusual will of God."[16]

Here, suddenly, out of the blue, as though it has just occurred to him and
he is quoting from memory, Martin Bucer cites Wessel Gansfort and accords
his authority more weight than that of the eminent theologians he has just
quoted, including Thomas Aquinas. Bucer then eruditely goes on to add
a non-Christian authority to the list: "Even Aristotle," he says, "holds that

9. *Comm. Rom.*, 334b. Cf. John Chrysostom, *In Epistolam ad Romanos homiliae.*
Homilia XIV, 5-6, MSG 60:529–32. Chrysostom thinks it wiser to refrain from questions here: "Non oportet hic quaerere sed sperare" (op. cit., 532).

10. Augustine, *De civitate dei, lib. XX, c. 16*, MSL 41:681–82; CChr 48:726–27.

11. *Simpliciter; Comm. Rom.*, 344a.

12. Thomas Aquinas, *Summa theologiae* 3, q.91, a.4.5, Art. 1: "respondeo dicendum
quod omnia corporalia propter hominem facta esse creduntur, unde et omnia dicuntur
ei subjecta."

13. *Comm. Rom.*, 344b.

14. Adspirare esse temporarium et esse aeternum (ibid.).

15. Fingit siquidem ex nihilo omnia: unde coelum et corpora coelestia non plus
habent ex se ut perpetua sint quam quae sunt ephèmera (ibid.).

16. A striking printing error. Johannes Rucherat von Wesel (d. 1481) was often
confused with Wessel Gansfort. Like Gansfort, he had a critical attitude toward ecclesiastical doctrine and practices (e.g., with regard to indulgences) (TRE, 17:150–53)
(Gustav Adolf Benrath).

natural science is not guided by a compelling necessity, since all its conclusions are based both on reason *and* the nature of things."[17]

Is Bucer really quoting Wessel Gansfort? There can be no doubt in the matter. Not only the content, but also Bucer's wording reveals strong parallels with Wessel. According to the latter, the distinction between nature and a miracle does not lie in a causal difference, but purely in what is ordinary and what is extraordinary.[18] I shall return to this matter below.[19]

Bucer elaborates still further on Wessel's statement. One should not base one's conclusions on "how things appear to be now."[20] It is a matter of piety to refer everything back to the will of God.[21] Read the Bible, he says, and do not try to tell God what he may and may not do. Where the creation is concerned, Bucer continues, pointing the finger at Thomas Aquinas, everything is entirely in God's hand.[22]

Wessel's statement about nature and miracles can be found in his treatise *De certissima et benignissima providentia Dei*.[23] As far as I know, this is the only passage from the oeuvre of the Dutch theologian—aside from his correspondence—that Martin Bucer cites explicitly. Has the former Dominican converted to the nominalist thinking of Wessel Gansfort, who was himself a convert to nominalism? I shall return to this question at the end of this chapter.

2. EXPLORATORY FORAYS

Wessel's Treatise *De Eucharistia*

The name Wessel Gansfort is inextricably linked with the controversy about the Eucharist that broke out in the early years of the Reformation. Martin Bucer did more than most to try to avert the effects of this dramatic rift within the Reformation camp. It was largely due to his efforts that the Concord of

17. *Comm. Rom.*, 344b. The idea Bucer expresses here is indeed found in Aristotle, especially in his *Metaphysica* E1, 1023b–1026a: "Knowledge of nature has to do with things that are in flux." I am grateful to Prof. A. P. Bos (Amsterdam) for helping me to find important examples of this statement in Aristotle.

18. M. Wesseli Gansfortii Groningensis . . . *Opera*. Facsimile of the Edition Groningen 1614, 715.

19. See section 4 below.

20. "Nequaquam convenire, ut ex eo solo concludamus quod nunc in rebus apparet" (*Comm. Rom.*, 344b).

21. "Esse pietatis omnia referre ad Dei voluntatem" (ibid.).

22. Op. cit., 345a.

23. *Opera*, 711–33.

Wittenberg was agreed upon in 1536.[24] A few scattered remarks in Bucer's correspondence reveal that Gansfort had made a deep impression on him. "I am amazed this man is not better known." This quotation comes from Bucer's letter to a certain "Germanus" in Fürfeld, written between October and December 1525.[25] Bucer includes Gansfort in the long line of theologians, stretching from Tertullian right up to Zwingli and Oecolampadius, who all teach that the bread is a symbol of the body of Christ. In this way, the faithful are offered the body of Christ. But this occurs through the Word, and this means that the mouth eats only the bread, whereas the spirit feeds on the body of Christ through faith.[26]

In this letter, Bucer sketches the evolution of his thinking about the presence of Christ in the Eucharist. This reveals that he rejects the *praesentia corporalis (carnalis)* in the Lord's Supper. His visit from Hinne Rode (before November 21, 1524) was decisive in this. As Bucer puts it: "In some respects this man acknowledges Luther as his master, but he owes more to Wessel Gansfort."[27] This calls to mind Luther's praise of Wessel in the early years of the Reformation, which is even more lavish: "If I had read this man before, it might have appeared to my enemies as though Luther had drawn everything from Wessel, so much do we breathe the one spirit."[28] But this most emphatically does not mean that Luther shared Wessel's views on the Eucharist! Let us not forget Albert Hardenberg's testimony in his *Vita Wesseli*. He reports that Wessel's works were collected by Cornelis Hoen, a lawyer in The Hague, and were published in print by Hinne Rode, Bucer's visitor, in 1521–23.[29] This same Hoen is the author of the celebrated treatise *Epistola christiana admodum* (1524/1525), which had such a decisive influence on the controversy concerning the Eucharist.[30] These are a few of the well-known historical facts.

In Bucer's numerous works about the Eucharist, however, I did not encounter Wessel Gansfort's name even once. In seeking the origins of the controversy about the Eucharist, all roads lead to Cornelis Hoen's famous treatise,

---

24. I. Hazlett, *The Development of Martin Bucer's Thinking on the Sacrament of the Lord's Supper in Its Historical and Theological Context 1523–1534* (theol. diss., 1975, Münster, 1977). See also *Wittenberger Konkordie (1536). Schriften zur Wittenberger Konkordie (1534–1537)*, ed. Robert Stupperich, Marijn de Kroon, and Hartmut Rodolph, BDS 6:1 (Gütersloh, 1988).

25. *Correspondance de Martin Bucer* (BCor), vol. 2, ed. Jean Rott (Leiden, 1989), no. 109, 53, ll. 78–79.

26. Op. cit., no. 114, 81, ll. 53–55: "das brot sey ein zeychen des leibs Cristi . . . vnd also esse der mundt nur das brodt, der geyst aber den leip Cristi durch den glauben."

27. Op. cit., no. 109, 53, ll. 77–78.

28. *Opera*, 854.

29. Hazlett (n. 24), 38–95.

30. *Zwingli Werke*, 4:512–19.

to Zwingli's interpretation of the words of institution, Carlstadt's stance in Wittenberg, and Luther's furious response to the sacramentarians' views. If one compares Hoen's *Epistola christiana admodum* (1525) with Wessel's views on the Eucharist, one finds two completely different ways of thinking. Wessel's reflections on the Eucharist are an expression of his vision of Christian life. He is not overly interested in doctrinal issues, focusing rather on what faith means for the believer's innermost being.[31] His treatise about the Eucharist is a concerted plea for internalization, a testimony to the brand of spirituality that was nurtured by the *Devotio moderna*. It is about the innermost self, about internal nourishment, spiritual nourishment, which is identical to faith. "Those who believe in him—that is, who eat his flesh."[32] Wessel uses a full palette of words to paint these inner activities: it is all about believing, holding in remembrance, discerning (again and again Wessel emphasizes the Vulgate's term *dijudicare*), loving, ruminating (*ruminari*, another key word in the terminology of the *Devotio moderna*), and so on, the author adds.[33] On one occasion, he formulates the essence very succinctly: *credendo, commemorando, considerando.*[34] "When I commemorate you, be you my worthy guest."[35] These features apply to celebrating the Eucharist, but they are equally characteristic of a true Christian life. The Christ held in remembrance here, in this life-filling celebration, is always *Christus traditus*, Christ who gave himself for us.[36] This has far-reaching consequences for each and every Christian; it cuts deep into the flesh: "In partaking in the Eucharist we eat and are eaten."[37]

It is understandable that the spiritual interpretation of the Eucharist in Wessel's treatise appealed greatly to Cornelis Hoen and like-minded Christians, but Wessel's writing is so individual and personal that it stands apart from the Reformation controversy about the Eucharist.[38]

31. See M. van Rhijn, *Studiën over Wessel Gansfort en zijn tijd* (Utrecht, 1933), 74–90, and idem, *Wessel Gansfort* (The Hague, 1917), 230–63.

32. *De sacramento Eucharistiae et audienda Missa; Opera*, 678. Cf. "Ergo credere est bibere sanguinem ejus" (700, *propositio* 9).

33. Op. cit., 677, 682, etc. Very extensively in *propositio* 32 (op. cit., 702). Cf. above, chap. 2, n. 153.

34. Op. cit., 675.

35. Op. cit., 661.

36. Op. cit., 660–63.

37. This is the heading of caput XIX: ". . . quod ejus participatione etiam sicut manducamus, ita et manducamur" (op. cit., 691).

38. The doctrine of transsubstantiation is not under discussion in Wessel's treatise. It is neither affirmed nor denied. The text adduced by B. J. Spruyt permits the conclusion only that Wessel professes the actual presence of Christ in the Lord's Supper ("*ipse enim adest . . .*" [op. cit., 695–96, cf. 673 and 690]). In Wessel's thinking, the body of the Lord is also present, for those who believe, outside the celebration of the Eucharist, even without the symbols of bread and wine (op. cit., 696). The word

Wessel's Treatise *De potestate ecclesiastica*

The links between Wessel's discussion of ecclesiastical power and Bucer's views on this subject (*potestas spiritualis*) are more concrete and easier to trace. In terms of content, this controversial theme of authority within the church is the most important field for my exploratory forays. Wessel's views are a razor-sharp, critical analysis of the exercise of authority in the church of his day.[39] His deliberations do not amount to a rejection of the papacy and hierarchical structures in themselves; this is certainly not the case. But Wessel's criticism of pope and prelates goes so deep that not a shred remains intact of the way in which these figures actually exercise their authority. If one is familiar with Bucer's extensive treatment of spiritual power in the church (*potestas spiritualis*) in his commentary on Romans 13, it is virtually impossible to read Wessel's treatise without being constantly reminded of Bucer's views.[40] The similarities do not extend to the theologians' style of writing, but certainly hold for the way in which both underpin their criticism. There is one instance in which it seems as though Bucer is directly reliant on Wessel, right down to his chosen wording—and this is a statement that has hitherto been seen as particularly characteristic of Bucer himself! In Wessel's words, the passage in question reads: "For after all, it is because of God that we believe the gospel, and because of the gospel that we believe the church and the pope; we do not believe the gospel because of the church."[41] The present exploratory forays will reveal that these words of Wessel's made a deep impression on Bucer, even if he formulates his views very differently from the Dutch theologian.

However, do these observations prove that Wessel Gansfort influenced Bucer's criticism of the functioning of those in authority in the church of his day? This question requires further investigation.

---

corporaliter, which Spruyt cites as evidence, occurs outside the context of transsubstantiation. Wessel himself fills in the context in which the word *corporaliter* should be read: "*Vbi duo vel tres fuerint congregati in nomine meo . . .*" (Matt. 18:20). See B. J. Spruyt, *Wessel Gansfort and Cornelis Hoen's Epistola Christiana: 'The Ring as a Pledge of my love,'* in *Wessel Gansfort (1419–1489) and Northern Humanism,* ed. F. Akkerman, G. C. Huisman, and A. J. Vanderjagt (Leiden, New York, Cologne, 1993), 133. Cf. also W. Janse, *Albert Hardenberg als Theologe. Profil eines Bucer-Schülers (†1574)* (Leiden, etc., 1994), 274–83. In Janse's view, the *proprium* of Wessel's Eucharistic theory lies "in der eigentümlichen Gleichzeitigkeit von körperlicher Präsenz und geistlicher Niessung von Christi Leib und Blut innerhalb und ausserhalb der Eucharistie . . ." (the peculiar simultaneity of bodily presence of, and spiritual feeding on, Christ's body and blood, both within and outside the Eucharist) (ibid., 275).

39. *Opera*, 748–71: *De dignitate et potestate ecclesiastica* (trans. chap. 2 above).

40. *Comm. Rom.*, 13:1–6; 477a–492, esp. 482–92.

41. *Opera*, 759. In other writings too, Wessel shows a penchant for such antithetical formulations. Cf. chap. 2, n. 4 above (in his treatises *De sacramento poenitentiae* [op. cit., 779], and *De causis incarnationis* [op. cit., 426–27]).

In considering this matter, I am guided by Bucer's exegesis of Romans 13, the central Bible passage about the governing authorities to which every person must be subject or, more precisely, by the *Quaestio* he raises in this context.[42] This *Quaestio* goes as follows: "Is the power that wields the sword on earth the highest power of all, to which everyone who lives on earth must be subject?[43] Bucer first explains where the highest constitutional power lies in the Europe of his day. In fact, this *Quaestio* is a lecture in constitutional law. Bucer had a particularly good understanding of political relations, and was by far the most astute politician of the major figures of the Reformation. He answers the question by positing that the highest jurisdiction (*merum imperium*)[44] is not exclusively in the hands of the emperor; other "powers" too have a share in this jurisdiction.[45] All power comes from God, including the power of the magistracy of a free imperial city (i.e., Strasbourg, Bucer's own city!).

But Bucer is not interested simply in discussing issues of constitutional law. He has other things in mind than providing insight into the power structures of the Holy Roman Empire. His main concern is the gospel. The real question is, What is the prime concern of a government supported by God? Answer: "The highest jurisdiction (*merum imperium*) should institute policies that ensure that its subjects' Christian worship is properly looked after."[46] Or, more succinctly: "The government's prime concern must be true religion."[47] This position has very wide-ranging implications. The theologian's attitude seems absurd and objectionable, certainly for most twenty-first-century readers, for whom a link of this kind between religion and the state seems threatening and unacceptable. Here one should also mention a telling statement in which Bucer even goes one step further, and this too is directly connected with this Bible passage: everyone, the Scriptures say (πᾶσα ψυχή), must obey this [secular] authority, also in matters of religion. And this includes priests and monks![48] This sounds rather more acceptable and understandable to us.

And now the true point of the discussion comes to light: Bucer wants to mobilize the secular authorities to call the clergy to order, precisely where society's most precious value is concerned: the Christian faith. He is going to stage an attack on the clergy's privileged status, the detested *clerical immunity*.

42. *Comm. Rom.*, 482b–492a.
43. Op. cit., 482b.
44. Op. cit., 483b–484a.
45. Rom. 13:1.
46. Op. cit., 484a.
47. Op. cit., 489b.
48. Op. cit., 484a. Drawing on Chrysostom, *In Epistolam ad Romanos homilia. Homilia XXIII*: MSG 60:613–15 (esp. 615).

Having thus carefully prepared the way and set in place sound foundations, Bucer opens his attack on the spiritual authority of the clergy of his day. Precisely because the highest power has been neglecting its highest duty—care of religion—clerics, popes, and prelates have had free rein and have built up a spiritual jurisdiction that is fatal for Christendom and calamitous for the gospel of Christ. "The entire estate of the clergy derives its raison d'être from the pope of Rome; he prevents rulers and the magistracy from taking proper care of religion."[49] "Do they exercise spiritual authority? Yes, but they are inspired by the mind of the devil, and not the spirit of Christ."[50] Bucer fulminates against the privileged, separate status (immunity) of the clergy: "What is it other than a licence for licentiousness, to do with impunity all those things that God has forbidden?"[51]

Edification and Piety

What, one may ask, is true spiritual power (*potestas spiritualis*)? The answer: "It is a gift of the spirit of Christ effectively to weed out sinful practices among humankind and to sow, protect, and nurture *pietas*."[52] In other words, "It is the power of the Spirit, the power of the Word to be effective in building up [the church]."[53]

Constructiveness/edification and piety: these are the key words that Bucer's roundabout argument has eventually brought us to. He has had to travel a long and laborious path, but nonetheless a fascinating one, to reach this radical conclusion.

Wessel Gansfort follows a completely different path, but surprisingly enough he arrives at the same destination, reaches the same conclusions. The central Bible passage in Wessel's criticism of those in authority in the church is Matthew 23. "The scribes and the Pharisees sit on Moses' seat; therefore, do whatever they teach you and follow it; but do not do as they do, for they do not practice what they teach."[54] But Wessel also refers to other passages of Scripture, including the comment about the authorities in Romans 13 that serves as the starting point for Bucer's discourse.[55]

So how does Wessel interpret Paul's words? People in positions of authority, he argues, can err, whether their authority be religious or secular. They can even drag down their subjects into fatal error. For the people too may

49. *Comm. Rom.*, 484b.
50. Op. cit., 487a.
51. Op. cit., 486a.
52. Op. cit., 486b.
53. Op. cit., 490a.
54. Matt. 23:2–3. Cf. above, chap. 2, passim.
55. Cf. chap. 2 above, /768–69/.

have blood on their hands if they give their tacit consent.[56] "The apostle's words about authority should be understood, as he himself puts it slightly differently elsewhere, to mean that there is no authority except insofar as it is constructive. For so long as authority is constructive, it comes from God; if it is not constructive, the person who is constructive through resistance has received the power to resist from God."[57] Wessel's wording may be problematic from a grammatical point of view, but his meaning is crystal clear. I know no other text from the Reformation period that so clearly and so radically advocates the right to put up resistance, using Romans 13 as its basis, as Wessel Gansfort does here. Wessel's views on the right to put up resistance were known to the authorities in Strasbourg. They were propagated fiercely by Johann von Wijck, syndic of that town.[58]

The continuation of Wessel's discussion is also worth repeating in this context. Being constructive comes from God, and the one who is more constructive has higher authority. In terms of true power, then, Paul stands higher than Peter, Bernard higher than Innocent or Eugene, and Francis higher than Honorius.[59]

Wessel explains Romans 13 in the light of 2 Corinthians 10:8, which speaks of "authority, which the Lord gave for building you up and not for tearing you down." For Martin Bucer too, 2 Corinthians 10 is a central passage when it comes to explaining *potestas spiritualis* in biblical terms. This term "constructiveness/edification" (*aedificatio*, οικοδομὴ) is a key term in Bucer's theology. I have explored it in greater detail elsewhere.[60]

In this context, one must mention a second concept that plays a fundamental role for both Wessel Gansfort and Martin Bucer, precisely in the discussion about the functioning of spiritual authority in the church: the concept of *pietas*. In Bucer's thinking, this concept is the quintessential ethical norm, but it also summarizes the very essence of his theology.[61] It is scarcely surprising that this concept of *pietas* plays a crucial role in understanding what spiritual power is, in a negative sense, but above all in a positive one: "sowing *pietas*, protecting and nurturing it."[62] In his further elaboration of what

---

56. Op. cit., /769/.
57. Ibid.
58. For Bucer's views on *potestas spiritualis*, see M. de Kroon, *Studien*, 108–13. Cf. 112, n. 144. For Johann von Wijck's document concerning the right to resist, see op. cit. 6, n. 19 and 152–53.
59. See above, chap. 2, /766–67/, n. 155, and /769/.
60. De Kroon, *Studien*, 127–29.
61. Op. cit., 114–22: Die ethische Norm *pietas*.
62. *Comm. Rom.*, 486b.

spiritual power should really be, both terms, "constructiveness" and "*pietas*," blend together harmoniously. What those in true spiritual authority should do is to build up their subjects in *pietas*.[63] This is the only true "power" in the church of Christ. And this is the only "power" that can have any justification in the church.

Does the concept of *pietas* also play a role in Wessel Gansfort's thinking about spiritual power in the church? As far as I am aware, the significance of this concept in Wessel's theology has not yet been the subject of detailed research. This would require a separate study, and is beyond the scope of the present work. Only such research will tell, but with the necessary caveats, the answer to the question posed above must be a clear affirmative. *Pietas* plays a striking role in Wessel's theology, and on one occasion is even quite literally key. The heading of the passage that describes this key role is this: "If a pope is not constructive, he is engaged only in dangerous endeavors."[64] The way our prelates go about their work, Wessel laments, has nothing to do with the keys to the kingdom of heaven. Their key is that of the Pharisees: they cannot go in themselves, and they obstruct others from entering. As Wessel puts it: "No matter how much they fight for the key to power—and fight they certainly do—all their efforts are in vain. For in fact the true key to the kingdom of heaven, a much greater and truer one, is the key of piety. Without this key, the key of power can accomplish nothing. And wherever this key [of piety] is used, it is always joined to the key of power."[65] This is Wessel at his best: pithy and profound.

Religious Office as a Position

With these two key terms, edification and *pietas*, the two theologians lay firm foundations for a sound use of *potestas spiritualis*, of "power" in the church, that is in line with biblical teachings. Both stand squarely on these foundations, and from this base they voice their criticism of the way in which ecclesiastical office has come to function. A new vision of what religious office should mean shines through: it must develop from an *ordo* into an *officium*; what was formerly a status now becomes a job description. The two theologians' hard-hitting criticism of the clergy of their day effectively amounts to advocating a new understanding of religious office. Two quotations will illustrate the similarity of their views:

63. Ibid. (n. 60).
64. See above, chap. 2, /767/.
65. Op. cit., /768/.

Wessel: "If a pastor does not graze his sheep, he is not a pastor."[66]

Bucer: "[If the bishops of Rome want to be seen as the successors to the apostle Peter,] they must demonstrate and prove this by grazing Christ's sheep."[67]

Wessel is even more radical than Bucer in the demands he makes on the functioning of ecclesiastical office, as he views all power in the church in terms of a reciprocal agreement. "Power in the church is like an agreement between a physician and his patient, i.e., it consists of a contract between two parties."[68] This idea is absent from Bucer's thinking.

Both Wessel and Bucer show awareness of the geographical limitations to the exercise of true pastoral care and spiritual authority. Both of them favor local church structures, "frontline" pastoral care. Partly for this reason, Bucer regards the title *episcopus universalis* for the bishop of Rome as an impossible pretension; Pope Gregory is his star witness to this effect.[69]

Wessel takes a similar stance on the matter, and expresses his views clearly and unambiguously: "In the face of general opinion concerning the supreme power of the bishop of Rome, one can adduce the following: it is impossible for one man to know the boundaries of the entire globe. They have never been charted by a cosmographer. So how can he (the pope of Rome) pass judgment on people that he does not know? How can he pass judgment on people's faith, when he does not even speak their language? The Holy Spirit reserved for itself the task of promoting unity in the church, making it grow, and giving it life."[70] This quotation prompts all sorts of questions from a modern point of view (in light of the process of globalization), but was equally relevant in Wessel's day.

Martin Bucer too advocates the decentralization of pastoral care. "The pastoral services of the one may reach further than those of another. But no one man is capable of providing pastoral care everywhere."[71] "Who can truly take care of all the souls under his charge . . . even in one little town? Can one ever really achieve this?"[72]

---

66. See above, chap. 2, /753/.

67. Martin Bucer, *Furbereytung zum Concilio* (1533); BDS 5:326. For Bucer's views on ecclesiastical office, see W. van 't Spijker, *The Ecclesiastical Offices in the Thought of Martin Bucer* (Leiden, etc., 1996), esp. 29–34 ("Bucer's Criticism of Rome's Static Concept of Office"), and 383–91 ("Ministry and Ministries").

68. See above, chap. 2, /752/ and /755/.

69. *Comm. Rom.*, 490b.

70. *Opera*, 779. From *De sacramento poenitentiae*, par. *Fides nostra non homini, sed Deo obligatur.*

71. *Comm. Rom.*, 490b.

72. Op. cit., 491a.

Bucer knows what he is talking about: he knows from experience all about pastoral care in practice. And in 1538, two years after the publication of his commentary on Romans, he explicitly called attention to the office of the pastor. In his treatise *Von der waren Seelsorge* [Of true pastoral care] (1538),[73] he urges the believers to respect their local pastors, to show them regard and obedience, love and esteem. Ultimately, it is all about Christ. "You must desire to show obedience to Christ, not to the pastors. Should you obey the latter? Yes, as long as they are servants of the Lord, and not servants of men or of themselves." In the margins, one finds the comment: "*Man suchet eyn gehorsame Christi und nit der diener*" [One must strive for obedience to Christ, not to his servants].[74] The author's reverence for clerical office is high. Now that the Reformation has taken root in Strasbourg, he wishes to provide a firm theological basis for the position of the pastors, not only with regards to their parishioners but precisely also with a view to the numerous clashes with the magistracy of the town when it comes to imposing ecclesiastical discipline.[75]

However, the criteria devised to keep the pope and prelates up to the mark apply equally to pastors on the ground. Wessel applies the same yardstick to the latter group, in almost identical wording, as in his discussion of the jurisdiction of the pope in Rome. "If, therefore, the people place their faith in their pastor, if it is truly a matter of faith, then the people believe for this reason: because the pastor's faith is in accordance with the gospel. If the people thought that the pastor was not preaching in accordance with the gospel, they would not have faith in him."[76] Wessel believes in the independence of mind of ordinary churchgoers. The shepherd is appointed to graze the Lord's flocks. But this flock that is to be grazed is capable of thinking and making its own judgments. So it is not entirely at the mercy of the pastor, as though one could ask nothing of it other than obedience. If a shepherd does *not* graze his flock, he is not worthy of the name. Then he is effectively "out of order," and the sheep are not obliged to obey him.[77]

3. ANTITHETICAL FORMULATIONS

I have just quoted a statement of Bucer's that has a ring of Wessel Gansfort about it: "*Man suchet eyn gehorsame Christi und nit der diener*." These sorts of outspoken aphorisms by the critical Gansfort can be seen as variations on

73. BDS 7:67–245.
74. Op. cit., 237, 17–20.
75. Op. cit., 69–84.
76. See chap. 2, /758/.
77. Op. cit., /753/.

the statement that seems to have made such an impression on Bucer: "It is because of God that we believe the gospel, and because of the gospel that we believe the church and the pope. We do not believe the gospel because of the church."[78]

I now propose to examine antithetical statements of this kind in Bucer's oeuvre, formulations that are reminiscent of Wessel. It is not my intention to give an exhaustive list, but rather to provide a representative illustration. Let me point out first, however, that these formulations must all be seen as a response to the famous dictum of Augustine's on which the present work centers: "I would not believe the gospel, were it not that the authority of the Catholic Church compels me to do so."[79] With this translation, I deliberately sidestep the discussion about whether the original Latin version read *commoveret* or *commoneret*. In fact, it makes little difference to the meaning of the statement as a whole. On a few occasions, Bucer even uses Augustine's statement as ammunition against the church father himself. And he cites it against Martin Luther several times.

This manner of speaking, precisely in response to Augustine's words, did indeed find strong echoes in Bucer, even in his earliest writings. Let me illustrate this with a few quotations from Martin Bucer, in chronological order:

1. Bucer's treatise *Dass D. Luthers und seiner nachfolger leer . . . christlich und gerecht ist* (1523–24)[80] reveals his familiarity with Augustine's statement. In discussions about the authority of the ecclesiastical hierarchy, church fathers, popes, and councils, as opposed to the testimony of the Scriptures, the opponents of the Reformation also cite Augustine's words: "They weigh in against me with Augustine's statement: I would not believe the gospel if I did not believe the church."[81] As yet, however, Bucer does not respond with criticism along Wessel Gansfort's lines.

2. This changes in Bucer's *Handel mit Cunrat Treger* (October 20, 1524). Here Bucer posits: "We believe in God and in Christ, not in the church."[82] And Bucer goes on to quote Augustine's famous statement. Here he quotes

78. Op. cit., /759/.
79. Augustine, *Contra epistulam manichaei quam vocant 'fundamenti'* 5, 6; MSL 42:176 (= CSEL 25:1, 197, 22s).
80. BDS 1:310, 344.
81. Op. cit., 314, 2–3. Cf. ibid., n. 28 and 29. "Mer wirfft man . . . engegen den spruoch Augustini: ich glaubt dem Evangelio nit, ich glaubet dan der kirchen."
82. BDS 2:92, 31. "Wir seind Gott und christgläubig, nit kirchgläubig." If this fine formulation was indeed inspired by Wessel, it would mean that Bucer was already familiar with Wessel's *Opera* before Hinne Rode visited him in Strasbourg at the end of November 1524. Cf. BCor 2:53, n. 13 and op. cit., 1:296, n. 30. For the editions of Wessel's writings, see C. Augustijn, *Wessel Gansfort's Rise to Celebrity*, in *Wessel Gansfort*, 3–22. Cf. also J. V. Pollet, *Martin Bucer. Études sur la correspondance* 1, 2 (Paris, 1958, 1962), 1:12–18 (*Martin Bucer à Martin* [Germanus] [1526]).

the second clause correctly ". . . were it not that the authority of the universal church admonishes me to do so."[83] And he responds to the church father's words as follows: "I do not accord Augustine's words too much weight, because ultimately it is Christ I must believe in, and not Augustine."[84] And a little further on, he puts it even more starkly: "It is much better to abandon Augustine than Christ."[85]

3. The next allusion to Augustine's statement can be found in Bucer's first publication about the Eucharist, *De Caena Dominica* (1524).[86] Here Bucer comments on Romans 10:17 ("faith comes from what is heard"), stating pithily that faith does indeed come from what is heard, but not "from hearing the words of the church, but those of Christ."[87] Bucer explicitly situates the celebration of the Lord's Supper in the context of faith and the covenant. And he does so in a formulation that is clearly reminiscent of the idiom of Wessel Gansfort, and thus also of the latter's discussion about Augustine's words and the relationship between faith and the authority of the church. This did not escape the attention of the editor of *De Caena Dominica*.[88] The unmistakable reference to Wessel—the words "not of the church, but of Christ"—is surprising and highly significant.

4. These themes also play a role in Bucer's *Berner Disputation* (1528). Here, interestingly enough, God and Martin Luther are viewed in opposition, but again the context is the relationship between ecclesiastical authority (here represented by Luther), on the one hand, and the word of God, on the other. With all due respect for Luther, Bucer says: "We should believe in God, and not in Luther;[89] and we rejoice that the Father has entrusted the last judgment to his Son, not to Luther, and equally not to the pope."[90]

5. Augustine's famous text is discussed by Bucer yet again in the Apology of his *Confessio Tetrapolitana* (1531).[91] Here too, Paul's words about faith coming from what is heard (Rom. 10:17) are the immediate cue for the discussion. And here too, Bucer's wording has echoes of the opposition that is so characteristic of Wessel Gansfort's theological thinking. "Faith comes from

83. BDS 2:94, 20–22: "Ich glaubte der kirchen [!] nit, wo mich nit ermante das ansehen der gemeyen Kirchen." The slip of the pen "kirchen" (instead of "Evangelio") was not noted by the editor.
84. Op. cit., 100, 9–10. ". . . dann ich christgläubig und nit Augustingläubig sein soll" (ibid., 10).
85. Ibid., 27–28. "Es ist vil besser Augustinum dann Christum zuo verlassen."
86. *Martini Buceri Opera Latina* (BOL) (Leiden, 1982), 1:1–58.
87. Op. cit., 30, 26–27. ". . . non verborum ecclesiae, sed Christi."
88. Marc Lienhard. Cf. ibid., n. 57.
89. BDS 4:82–3, 36–1. "Wie wir ouch Gott und nit Luter glöubig sin söllend."
90. Ibid., 83, 5–6: ". . . Christo und nit dem Luter, wie ouch nit dem Bapst. . . ."
91. BDS 3:194–318.

what is heard. It is based on the word of God. For this reason, each person must acknowledge that it is God who says what he must believe. Otherwise he would believe in the church rather than in God."[92]

6. When Bucer addresses the Council of Augsburg in 1533 on behalf of the preachers, he again constructs an opposition between God and Luther, and with him all others who proclaim the faith: "It is God we must believe in, and not Luther or any human being."[93]

7. In Bucer's *Dialogi*, finally, written in 1535, Habakkuk 2:4 ("the righteous live by their faith"; cf. Rom. 1:17) prompts Bucer to formulate in true Wesselian style: ". . . otherwise we would believe in people, and not in God."[94] Again the central issue is faith, but this quotation reveals the real basis of the opposition, from which all these criticisms of the words of the church and its representatives ultimately derive: the relationship between God and man.

Can we posit, on the basis of the above survey, that Martin Bucer's theology shows echoes of Wessel Gansfort's antithetical formulation in answer to Augustine's famous words? For me, this is the inevitable conclusion. Here we must remember the Bucer is not generally renowned for his style. In the wordy mass of his long, complex, and dense sentences, these pithy, antithetical phrases sparkle and stand out, in the best sense of the word.

Moreover, the conclusion is strengthened if we compare Bucer's wording with the ways in which other Reformation theologians respond to Augustine's statement. The controversy about how to interpret Augustine's words about the authority of the church dates from the very beginning of the Reformation and is reflected in Luther's earliest writings.[95] I have examined the passages in which Luther addresses Augustine's dictum, as well as the (no fewer than nine) places where Calvin alludes to the *Epistula fundamenti*.[96] Zwingli is the only one of the Reformers to reject Augustine's words without much ado. An

---

92. Op. cit., 229–30. ". . . sunst glaubet er der Kirchen und nit Gott" (ibid., 229, 21).

93. *Archiv St.-Thomas* (Strasbourg) 38 (20,1), no. 21, f. 365b (Oct. 11, 1533). "Wir müssen gothes, nit Luthers oder einige menschen gleubigen sien."

94. BDS 6:2, 57, 30–1. ". . . Sunst waere men menschen—und nit Gotsgleubig."

95. Cf. Weimarer Ausgabe (WA) 2:429ff. (*Resolutiones super propositionibus suis Lipsiae disputatis*. WA 6:560, 31–561, 33 (*De captivitate*), and WA 10, II, 89, 6-90 (*Von menschenlehre zu meiden*). See also above, chap. 2, section 3 (Excursus).

96. For the passages that demonstrate Calvin's familiarity with Augustine's statement, see L. Smits, *Saint Augustin dans l'oeuvre de Jean Calvin*, 2 vols. (Assen, 1956–58), 2:188. Calvin competently discusses the context in which Augustine's words should be understood. He thinks it is possible to express the meaning of the church in a single word: εἰσαγωγή, meaning to introduce to faith, bid/invite to faith. See M. de Kroon, *Augustinus*' Epistula fundamenti *in de uitleg van Johannes Calvijn*, in *Sola Gratia. Bron voor de Reformatie en uitdaging voor nu*, ed. A. van den Beek and W. M. van Laar (Zoetermeer, 2004), 70–86.

article by Bakhuizen van den Brink was enlightening for this aspect of my research, especially on Melanchthon's interpretation of Augustine.[97] All the Reformation theologians mentioned here took issue in some way with Augustine's dictum, and yet not one of them demonstrates the antithetical structure that is so characteristic of Bucer's wording here. And, let me add, Bucer is also the only one to quote the second part of Augustine identically to Wessel, that is, equally incorrectly.[98] These arguments on the basis of literary style reinforce the conclusion that the well-known Reformer of Strasbourg was indeed influenced by Wessel Gansfort.

At the level of content, the strong similarities revealed by the comparative analysis between Wessel Gansfort and Martin Bucer in regard to the concept of *potestas spiritualis* are the most revealing. For both theologians, the concepts of *constructiveness* and *pietas*—or, all rolled into one, being constructive through *pietas*—constitute the decisive criterion in assessing the legitimacy of the religious hierarchy in the church. This fundamental similarity is also the root of both theologians' understanding of the true meaning of ecclesiastical office. Effectiveness is key. However, it remains possible that Wessel Gansfort is merely one of the many to voice a general tide of criticism about the exercise of authority in the late-medieval church. These waves may also have reached Martin Bucer, perhaps as early as his schooldays in Schlettstadt.[99]

In the case of the quotation in Bucer's commentary on Romans 8:18, however, it is a very different story.[100] As stated above, this is the only time Bucer cites Wessel Gansfort explicitly. Here Wessel's influence, on both the form and the content of Bucer's text, is clear for all to see. And the theological point at issue in this part of the commentary is a very important one too: the question of the restoration of all creation. Bucer here shifts to a nominalist perspective, and he calls Wessel, himself a convert to nominalism, as his witness! This proof that Bucer is familiar with Wessel's work comes relatively late in the eminent Strasbourger's career—in 1536. Bearing this in mind, and in light of Bucer's insatiable thirst for knowledge and astonishing intellectual abilities,[101] it seems more than likely that he knew Wessel's oeuvre in

97. J. N. Bakhuizen van den Brink, *Traditio in de reformatie en het katholicisme in de zestiende eeuw. Voordrachten voor de Koninklijke Nederlandse Akademie van Wetenschappen* (1952). For the meaning of Augustine's dictum in the fifteenth century, see H. A. Oberman, *The Harvest of Medieval Theology: Gabriel Biel and Late Medieval Nominalism* (Cambridge, 1963), 369ff., 385ff.

98. See n. 81 above.

99. Cf. Greschat, op. cit. (n. 8), 19–23 (*Die Lateinschule*).

100. *Comm. Rom.*, 344b.

101. M. de Kroon, *Martin Bucer und Johannes Calvin. Reformatorische Perspektiven. Einleitung und Texte* (Göttingen, 1991), 235–48 ("Martin Bucers Physiognomie"). Cf. n. 82 above.

its entirety. This further strengthens the conclusion—with hindsight, so to speak—that the Alsatian Reformer was influenced by the Dutch theologian.

4. "NATURE IS . . . THE WILL OF GOD."

By quoting from Wessel's *De certissima et benignissima providentia Dei*,[102] Bucer seems to be choosing in favor of nominalism. To understand this quotation correctly, it is important to take the context of Wessel's statement into account. It occurs in his exegesis of Matthew 6:25–34, where Christ urges us to entrust all our worries to God, who takes our cares upon him.[103] Wessel detects a certain contradiction between this Father's care and the independent responsibility of human beings, who are called to be fruitful: "But surely a good field and a good tree bring forth good fruit?"[104] This must mean that that which is created has its own causation. But is this not at odds with the words of the Scripture, which urges us to give our worries to God? "This contradiction," Wessel continues, "can quickly be resolved if we replace the word 'cause' with 'prompt,' so that it is really God who brings everything about; he alone genuinely operates causally." "The secondary causes are indeed true causes, but comparatively speaking they are only prompts, which means that we can worthily cast all our cares onto him." "In fact, the secondary causes are contributory causes, in accordance with the words of John [14:12]: 'the one who believes in me will also do the works that I do and, in fact, will do greater works than these.' But he will do these works under the one who creates them, as without him he can do nothing."[105]

God and humanity both create things, both are credited with causality, but how exactly this cooperation hangs together remains obscure, no matter how carefully Wessel chooses his words. Then follows the conclusion that Bucer quotes. Given its importance, I shall quote it in full again:

> Nature is nothing other than the will of God. If nature is nothing other than the will of God expressing itself through the laws of the ordinary, and a miracle is the will of that same God transcending the boundaries of what is ordinary, then it becomes clear that nature and miracles must be distinguished from one another not by any difference in cause, but merely in what is ordinary and what is not.[106]

102. *Opera*, 714–15.
103. Cf. Matt. 7:17.
104. *Opera*, 714.
105. "Sed sub eo faciente faciet; quia sine eo nihil potest."
106. Ibid., 714–15.

Bucer summarizes Wessel's words as follows: "Nature is nothing other than the ordered will of God; a miracle is the extraordinary will of God.[107]

I give the context of Wessel's statement at length to show how his definition "works." Wessel is disturbed by the opinion of some people that God is not at work in all things. He refers approvingly and admiringly to Francis of Assisi, who approaches all creation with "brotherly affection."[108] Whether Wessel's view of Francis is a valid one is not relevant here. What matters is that this text is a very apt illustration of the religious foundations, the piety, that underlie Wessel Gansfort's theological thinking.

5. WESSEL'S PRAISE OF FRANCIS OF ASSISI

Francis has penetrated to the hidden secrets of nature

Magnificently and penetratingly	Grandi et alto considerationis oculo
Francis gazed deep into the secrets of nature,	Franciscus penetravit in abdita naturae
When, as a loving brother,	quando universam creaturam
He enfolded all creation in his embrace,	fraterno adfectu complectebatur
The fire he called "My brother,"	ignem fratrem appellans
The lark, "O sister mine";	et alaudam sororem
The fire and the sun "my brothers both"	ignem et solem fratres,
Arisen from the same God and Father.	tanquam ab eodem Deo Patre ortas;
Knowing this, he did not dare	unde non in illas dominium vendicare
To enforce dominion over them.	audebat,
All he would do was invoke their aid	sed auxilium tantum postulare praesumebat.
That trembling of the reverent soul	Magis autem augebitur
Will grow and grow,	trepidatio ista reverentis animi
The more we see God at work in all:	si deum in omnibus operantem aspiciamus:
In fire, the heat,	in igne calefacientem,
In sun, the light,	in sole lucentem,
That warms, that broods, that germinates.	ferventem, foventem, germinantem,
God's creatures are not slaves to us,	ut non tam nobis creaturae subserviant,

107. *Comm. Rom.*, 344b: "Etenim natura rerum nihil aliud est, ut pie sanctus ille vir Ionnes Wesselus scripsit, quam voluntas Dei ordinata: ut miraculum voluntas dei insolens."

108. "Fraterno affectu" (*Opera*, 714). The language Wessel uses to express his admiration for Francis of Assisi is poetic. The translation attempts to do some justice to this special piece of writing.

Rather the Creator	quam creator suo iussu cuncta nobis
Sets all before us,	praestet.
Subject to his will.	
If we remembered this	Hoc si attente in omnibus
	adverteremus,
In all we do,	non tam insolenter nobis regnum
We would not enforce our rule so	vindicaremus.
shamelessly.	
There are those, though,	Hunc vero perpetuae pietatis adfectum
Who think God instituted all things	supprimunt, suffocant, perimunt,
To act on their own,	qui sic putant res
And not God in them.	Deum instituisse,
These people suppress, suffocate,	ut ipsae res agant,
and destroy	
This attitude of lasting respect.	non Deum in eis;
And yet God works in them indeed,	cum tamen Deus in eis agentibus [agit]
As they work.	
Like the light shining in colors,	quemadmodum lux in colore
Lustrous and shimmering.	lustrante vel rutilante.

The penultimate couplet clearly has a polemic undertone. Here the "nominalist" Wessel Gansfort is taking a swipe at the followers of the *via antiqua*, who cannot accept that God is at work in all things, including human beings: "Man is at work under him who is at work in all things."[109]

6. CONCLUDING REMARKS

A. For the Thomist Martin Bucer, the relationship between the prime cause and the efficient cause was not in the least problematic. Both in his *Quaestio de praedestinatione* (prompted by Rom. 8:29) and in his *Conciliatio* (prompted by Rom. 2:6 and 3:10), he had used Thomist causality theory in commenting on the same Pauline epistle, referring to Aquinas's *Summa theologiae* 1, q.23.[110]

Why, then, does he resort here to Wessel's nominalist-sounding definition of the difference between nature and miracles? Simply because this best suits his interpretation of Romans 8:18! The restoration of creation, the new heaven and new earth do not need to be delineated and determined within

---

109. Ibid. Cf. the description given by Wessel (*Opera*, 715): "Si natura nihil aliud quam voluntas Dei consuetudinis lege regulata et miraculum ejusdem Dei voluntas praeter solitum, liquet non causarum diversitate, naturam a miraculo secernendam, verum solito et insolita tantum."

110. De Kroon, op. cit. (n. 101), 19–57 and 59–117.

the boundaries of nature as we now know it. No, these boundaries have their origin in the will of God, which is free and unbounded. This same will is the origin both of the "ordinary" (nature) and the "extraordinary" (miracles). This is the reason that Bucer here switches to a nominalist-sounding manner of theological argumentation.

But at the same time, it is evident that for him both ways, the *via antiqua* and the *via moderna*, are indeed merely ways, not an end in themselves. The true mainspring behind his thinking is *pietas*, and he states this repeatedly precisely in these pages of his commentary.[111]

Moreover, the question of whether Wessel Gansfort should be characterized as a nominalist on the grounds of his statement about nature and miracles is equally open to discussion. Oberman quite rightly reads Wessel's definition of nature and miracles as a reference to the well-known pair in nominalist thinking, *potentia absoluta/ordinata*.[112] But research into the criteria by which one might distinguish between theological schools of thought in the late Middle Ages has highlighted precisely that such criteria are difficult to pin down. Martin Bucer himself proves to be a surprising example of this from the Reformation period.

Wessel himself gives us reason enough to take his nominalist leanings with a grain of salt. Even his "conversion" to nominalism is questionable. While studying in Paris (1458–60?), Wessel began with the *Reales*, the theological path of high scholasticism (*via antiqua*), represented particularly by Thomas Aquinas (d. 1274), then transferred his allegiances to the *Formales*, the preferred path particularly of Duns Scotus (d. 1308), before alighting on nominalism, a manner of theological thinking introduced by William of Occam (1347).[113] Laconically he tells us that he could not find a safer path than that of the nominalists, so he decided to stick with this school of thought.[114] He keeps an open mind in the matter, as statements such as the following show: "I will say it quite openly: if I believed that something was at variance with Scripture, I would transfer to the Formales or the Reales immediately. I have

111. *Comm. Rom.*, 344: "esse pietatis omnia referre ad voluntatem Dei."

112. H. A. Oberman, *Wessel Gansfort: 'magister contradictionis,'* in *Wessel Gansfort (1419–1489)*, 97–121, esp. 99–108.

113. See above, chap. 1, section 1. The *Formales* took their name from the expression *distinctio formalis a parte rei*, which expresses their view that reality itself holds the roots of the formal, i.e., specific differences (*distinctiones*) that our reason discerns in reality. This *distinctio formalis* plays a major role for Scotus, particularly in relation to the doctrine of the Trinity. His views place him effectively at the base of *realism* (the *via antiqua*). Cf. the thorough article by R. Seeberg in RE 5:62–75, as well as TRE 9:218–31 (Werner Dettloff).

114. *Opera*, ** 2–3. Cf. W. Janse, *Albert Hardenberg als Theologe*, 274: "Der Grundton seiner Gedanken bleibt realistisch und zwar albertistisch . . ." (The fundamental tone of his thinking remains realist or, more specifically, Albertist).

no strong principles in the matter."[115] Or: "If I do err, I do not worry all that much about this error, as long as it is conducive to piety. That will always bear fruit."[116] For Wessel, too, *pietas* is the all-important thing.

B. Has the discussion about Augustine's dictum reached its conclusion? For centuries, the words of the church father that play a central role in the present work have been constantly in the wings of the history of the church and theology. The brief reception history of the passage in chapter 1 gives just some impression of this influence. Wessel Gansfort's remarkable and critical interpretation of Augustine's statement made its own mark, on Martin Bucer at least. In this sense, Wessel can be viewed as a bridge: he passes on the words of a church father to the Reformation, adding his own critical interpretation along the way. And Bucer apparently had what it takes to pick up these signals. This is evident from the way he processes Wessel's antithetical formulations.

So has the last word been said on Augustine's statement? This seems extremely unlikely. For what Augustine puts forward here touches on the central core of Christian revelation. In traditional terms, what we are talking about is the relationship between Scripture and tradition. Put differently, it is that between the testimony itself and the people who bear witness to it (Thomas Netter).[117] Contemplating these matters is a sensitive and vulnerable issue, since this affects the very heart of revelation. In comparison with this, the "controversy of the ways" just mentioned seems merely a little light, if stimulating, mental gymnastics. Without a central testimony of substance, bearing witness degenerates into empty babbling. But without this bearing witness, the testimony itself must die out.

Augustine's words have a future. Does this also hold true of the interpretation that Wessel Gansfort and—in his footsteps—Martin Bucer gave to these words?

This future, I believe, has already begun.

---

115. *Opera*, 877.

116. Op. cit., 698. The studies of H. Braakhuis and M. Hoenen give a convincing demonstration of just how fluid and intangible the distinctions between nominalists, realists, and formalists are, in terms of the actual content of their doctrines. See *Wessel Gansfort (1419–1489)*, 30–43 and 71–96.

117. See above, chap. 1, section 5.

Abbreviations

BCor	*Correspondance de Martin Bucer*. Ed. J. Rott et al. Leiden, 1979–.
BDS	*Martin Bucers Deutsche Schriften*. Ed. R. Stupperich et al. Gütersloh, 1960–.
BOL	*Martini Buceri Opera Latina*. Ed. F. Wendel et al. Vol. 15, 1.2ff. Paris, Gütersloh, 1955–.
CChr	*Corpus Christianorum*. Turnhout, 1953–.
CIC	*Corpus Iuris Canonici*. Ed. Ae. Friedberg. 2 vols. 2nd ed. Graz, 1959.
CO	*Ioannis Calvini opera quae supersunt omnia*. 59 vols. (= *Corpus Reformatorum*, vols. 29–87). Brunswick and Berlin, 1863–1900.
Comm. Rom.	Martin Bucer. *Metaphrases et enarrationes perpetuae epistolarum D. Pauli Apostoli . . . Tomus primus. Continens metaphrasin et enarrationem in Epistolam ad Romanos*. Strasbourg, 1536.
CSEL	*Corpus Scriptorum Ecclesiasticorum latinorum*. Vienna, 1866–.
DRCH	*Dutch Review of Church History*.
DThC	*Dictionnaire de Théologie catholique*. Paris, 1909–50.
LdM	*Lexikon des Mittelalters*. Vols. 1–10. Munich, Zurich, 1980–.
LThK	*Lexikon für Theologie und Kirche*. Ed. M. Buchberger. 2nd ed. 1930–38. 3rd ed. 1957–.
Mansi	*Sacrorum conciliorum nova et amplissima collectio*. Ed. J. D. Mansi. Vols. 1–53. Florence, Paris, 1759–1927. Reprint Graz, 1960–62.
MSG	J. P. Migne. *Patrologiae cursus completus, series graeca*. Vols. 1–161. Paris, 1857–66.
MSL	J. P. Migne. *Patrologiae cursus completus, series latina*. Vols. 1–221. Paris, 1841–64.
Niermeyer	*Mediae latinitatis lexicon minus*. Rev. ed. Leiden, Boston, 2002.
Opera	*M. Wesseli Gansfortii Groningensis Opera*. Groningen, 1614. Reprint, 1966.
OS	*Johannis Calvini Opera Selecta*. Ed. P. Barth and G. Niesel. 5 vols. Munich, 1926–62.

RE	*Realenzyklopädie für protestantische Theologie und Kirche*. Leipzig, 1896–1909.
TRE	*Theologische Realenzyklopädie*. Berlin, New York, 1977–.
WA	*Martin Luthers Werke. Kritische Gesamtausgabe*. Weimar, 1883–.

Sources and Secondary Literature

Major Writers

Augustine
— *De civitate dei*; MSL 41; CChr 48.
— *De doctrina christiana*; MSL 34.
— *Contra epistulam Manichaei quam vocant fundamenti* 5, 6; MSL 42; CSEL 25, 1.
— *Contra Faustum Manichaeum*; CSEL 25.
— *De magistro*; MSL 42.
— *Tractatus in Psalmum LXIII*[64] 1–4; CChr 39.
— *De trinitate*; MSL 42.
— *De fide et symbolo*; MSL 40

Wessel Gansfort
— *Letter to magister Jacobus Hoeck, Dean of Naaldwijk* (Sept. 19, 1487 or 1488); *Opera*, 876–912.
— *De causis incarnationis*; *Opera*, 413–57.
— *De certissima et benignissima providentia Dei*; *Opera*, 711–33.
— *De dignitate et potestate ecclesiastica*; *Opera*, 748–71.
— *De sacra Eucharistia et audienda Missa*; *Opera*, 655–705.
— *De sacramento Poenitentiae*; *Opera*, 771–809.
— *Vita Wesseli Groningensis conscripta ab Alberto Hardenbergio S. Theologiae Doctore*; *sed mutila*; *Opera*, ** 1–3 .

Martin Bucer
— *Bucer to the Council of Augsburg* (Oct. 11, 1533); *Archiv St.-Thomas* (Strasbourg), 38 (20, 1), no. 21, f. 365b.
— *Letter to Martin* [Germanus in Fürfeld] (Oct.–Dec. 1525); BCor 2: no. 109, 50–54.
— *Letter to Luther* (Nov. 23, 1524); BCor 1: no. 83, 288–97.
— *Die Berner Disputation* (1528); BDS 4:15–160.
— *De Caena Dominica* (1524); BOL 1:1–58.
— *Comm. Rom.* (1536).
— *Confessio Tetrapolitana, Apologia* (1531); BDS 3:194–318.

— *Dass D. Luthers und seiner nachfolger leer . . . christlich und gerecht ist* (1523–24); BDS 1:310–44.
— *Das ym selbs* (1523); BDS 1:29–67.
— *Dialogi* (1535); BDS 6:2, 39–188.
— *Furbereytung zum Concilio* (1533); BDS 5:259–362.
— *Handel mit Cunrat Treger* (1524); BDS 2:15–173.
— *Von der waren Seelsorge . . .* (1538); BDS 7:67–245.
— *Wittenberger Konkordie* (1536). *Schriften zur Wittenberger Konkordie (1534–1537)*; BDS 6:1.

Other Sources

D'Ailly, Pierre, P. de Alliaco. *Utrum Petri Ecclesia Lege reguletur . . . Rege gubernetur*; in Jean Gerson. *Opera Omnia.* Ed. L. E. Dupin. Antwerp, 1706. 1:665–66, 691–92.

Aristotle (quoted from the edition of the Academia regia Borussica. Berlin, 1960–61).
— *Analytica posteriora*
— *Analytica priora*
— *Ethica Nicomachea*
— *Metaphysica*
— *Topica*

Bernard of Clairvaux
— *De consideratione*; MSL 182.
— *De gratia et libero arbitrio*; MSL 182 (Dutch trans.: Anton van Duinkerken [Willem Asselbergs], *Uren met St. Bernard.* Baarn, year unknown, 117–27).

Biel, Gabriel
— *Collectorium circa quattuor libros Sententiarum. Liber tertius.* Ed. Wilfridus Werbeck and Udo Hofmann. Tübingen, 1979.
— *Canonis misse Expositio.* Ed. Heiko A. Oberman and William J. Courtenay. Pars Prima. Wiesbaden, 1963.

Boniface VIII. [Bull] *Unam Sanctam*; in CIC *Extravagantes Communes. Lib. I, Tit. VIII.*

Calvin, John. *Institutio Christianae Religionis* (1559); OS 3–5.

Chrysostom, John
— *In Epistolam ad Romanos homiliae. Homilia XIV*, 5–6; MSG 60.
— *Homilia XXIII*; MSG 60.

Codex Iuris Canonici (edition of 1917), Freiburg i.B., Bonn, 1919.
— *Canon 80* (Dispensatio).
— *Canon 1409* (Beneficium ecclesiasticum).

CIC Decretum Gratiani
— Causa II, Quaestio VII, can. *Nos si incompetenter.*
— Distinctio XI, can. *Palam.*
— Distinctio XXII, can. *Sacrosancta.*
— Distinctio XL, can. *Si Papa.*

CIC Decretales Gregorii IX
— Lib. I, Tit. VI, *De electione, et electi potestate.*
— Lib. V, Tit. III, *De simonia.*

CIC Extravagantes Ioannis XXII, De Verborum significatione, Tit. XIV.
— Cap. III, *Ad conditorem canonum.*
— Cap. IV, *Cum inter nonnullos.*

Corpus Iuris Civilis, Novellae (vol. 3 of this Corpus). Ed. R. Schöll. Berlin, 1895.

Constitutio Frequens (Oct. 9, 1417) of the 39th session of the Council of Constance; *Mansi* 27:1159.

Gerson, Jean
— *De consiliis evangelicis; Opera omnia.* Ed. L. Du Pin. Antwerp, 1706. 2:669–81.
— *De mystica theologia.* Ed. André Combes. Lugano [1958].
— *De potestate ecclesiastica. Oeuvres Complètes.* Introduction, texte et notes by monseigneur Glorieux. Paris etc., 1960–68. Vol. 6. L'œuvre ecclesiologique. No. 282, 210–50.
— *Ad reformationem contra simoniam;* op. cit., no. 279.
— *Tractatus de simonia;* op. cit., no. 276.
— *Trilogus in materia schismatis;* op. cit., no. 264.

Gregory of Rimini, OESA. *Lectura super primum et secundum sententiarum.* Ed. A. Damasus Trapp, OESA, and Venicio Marcolino. Tomus I *Super primum, Prologus.* Ed. Willigis Eckermann, OESA. Collaborante Manfred Schulze. Berlin, New York, 1981. 20–22.

Hermann von Schildesche, OSA, Hermanni de Scildis. *Tractatus contra haereticos negantes immunitatem iurisdictionem sanctae ecclesiae.* Ed. Adolar Zumkeller. Würzburg, 1970.

Intern. Commentaar op de Bijbel. Ed. Averbode. 2 vols. Kok, Kampen, 2001.

Hoeck, Jacobus. *Brief aan magister Wessel Gansfort* (July 24, 1487 or 1488); *Opera,* 871–76.

Hoen, Cornelis. *Epistola christiana admodum* (1524/25); *Zwingli Werke* 4, 12–19.

Luther, Martin
— *De captivitate Babylonica ecclesiae, Praeludium* (1520); WA 6:484–573.
— *Von Menschenlehre zu meiden* (1520); WA 10 II:72–92.
— *Resolutiones super propositionibus Lipsiae disputatis* (1519); WA 2:391–435.

Pseudo-Augustinus. *De fide ad Petrum;* MSL 40.

Pseudo-Dionysius [Dionysius Areopagita]. *De Caelesti Hierarchia; De Ecclesiastica Hierarchia;* MSG 3, 4.

Rufinus. *Expositio symboli Apostolici* c. 36; MSL 21:373.

Thomas Aquinas. *Summa theologiae*. Ed. Turin, 1922.

Thomas [Netter] Waldensis carmelitae anglici. *Doctrinale antiquitatum fidei catholicae ecclesiae.* Ed. F. Bonaventura Blanciotti. Tomus primus. Venice, 1757.

Theologisch Woordenboek. 3 vols. Roermond, Maaseik, 1952, 1957, 1958.

William of Occam, Guillemus de Occam. *Dialogus de potestate papae et imperatoris. Compendium errorum Johannis XXII.* Turin, 1959. Reprint of the ed. Frankfurt, 1614.

Secondary Literature

Augustijn, C. *Wessel Gansfort's Rise to Celebrity.* In *Wessel Gansfort(1419–1489)*, 3–22.
Bakhuizen van den Brink, J.N. *Traditio in de reformatie en het katholicisme in de zestiende eeuw.* Voordrachten voor de Koniklijke Nederlandse Akademie van Wetenschappen, 1952.
Braakhuis, H. A. G., *Gansfort between Albertism and Nominalism.* In *Wessel Gansfort (1419–1489)*, 30–43.
Brecht, M. *Martin Luther. Sein Weg zur Reformation. 1483–1521.* 2nd ed. Stuttgart, 1983.
Feldmann, E. *Die 'Epistula Fundamenti' der nordafrikanischer Manichäer. Versuch einer Rekonstruktion.* Altenberge, 1987.
Fuhrmann, H., *Einladung ins Mittelalter.* 2nd ed. Munich, 2002.
Greschat, M., ed. *Gestalten der Kirchengeschichte* 4. Mittelalter II. Stuttgart, etc., 1983.
———. *Martin Bucer. Ein Reformator und seine Zeit.* Munich, 1990.
Hazlett, I. *The Development of Martin Bucer's Thinking on the Sacrament of the Lord's Supper in Its Historical and Theological Context 1523–1534.* Theol. Diss, 1975. Münster, 1977.
Histoire de Strasbourg. Sous la direction de Georges Livet et Francis Rapp. 1987.
Hoenen, M. J. F. M. *Albertistae, thomistae* und *nominales:* die philosophisch-historischen Hintergründe der Intellektlehre des Wessel Gansfort (†1489). In *Wessel Gansfort (1419–1489)*, 71–96.
Huizinga, J. *The Waning of the Middle Ages.* London, 1976.
Janse, W. *Albert Hardenberg als Theologe. Profil eines Bucer-Schülers (†1574).* Leiden, 1994.
Jungmann, J. A. *The Mass of the Roman Rite. Its Origins and Development.* Missarum Sollemnia. Trans. F. A. Brunner and Rev. Ch. K. Riepe. New York, etc., 1959.
Kroon, M. de. *Gerard Groote.* In Martin Greschat, ed., *Gestalten der Kirchengeschichte* 4. Mittelalter II (Stuttgart, etc.,1983), 234–50.
———. *Studien zu Martin Bucers Obrigkeitsverständnis. Evangelisches Ethos und politisches Engagement.* Gütersloh, 1984.
———. *Een van ons. Perspectief op verzoening.* Zoetermeer, 1999.
———. *Martin Bucer und Johannes Calvin. Reformatorische Perspektiven. Einleitung und Texte.* Göttingen, 1991.
Meer, F. van der. *Augustine the Bishop: the Life and Work of a Father of the Church.* Trans. B. Battershaw and G. R. Lamb. 1983.
Moolenbroek, J. van. *The Correspondence of Wessel Gansfort. An Inventory.* In *Dutch Review of Church History* 84 (2004).
———. *Wessel Gansfort as a Teacher at the Cistercian Abbey of Aduard. The Dismissal of Caesarius of Heisterbach's Dialogus Miraculorum.* In *Education and Learning in*

the Netherlands. 1400–1600, ed. K. Goudriaan et al. (Leiden, Boston, 2004), 113–32.

Oberman, H. A. *The Harvest of Medieval Theology. Gabriel Biel and Late Medieval Nominalism.* Cambridge, 1963.

———. *Wessel Gansfort: "magister contradictionis."* In *Wessel Gansfort (1419–1489)*, 97–121.

Oort, J. van. *Mani, Manichaeism and Augustine. The Rediscovery of Manichaeism and Its Influence on Western Christianity.* Tbilisi, 1998.

———. *Augustinus' Confessiones. Gnostische en christelijke spiritualiteit in een diepzinnig document.* Turnhout, 2002.

Pastor, L. von. *Geschichte der Päpste im Zeitalter der Renaissance von der Thronbesteigung Pius' II bis zum Tode Sixtus' IV.* Vol. II. Freiburg (Br.), 1925.

Posthumus Meyjes, G. H. M. *Jean Gerson. Apostle of Unity. His Church Politics and Ecclesiology.* Trans. J. C. Grayson. Leiden, etc., 1999.

———. *Quasi stellae fulgebunt. Plaats en functie van de theologische doctor in de middeleeuwse maatschappij en kerk.* Leiden, 1979.

Rapp, F. *Réformes et Réformation à Strasbourg. Eglise et société dans le diocèse de Strasbourg (1450–1525).* Paris[1974]. 281–318.

Rhijn, M. van. *Studiën over Wessel Gansfort en zijn tijd.* Utrecht, 1933.

———. *Wessel Gansfort.* The Hague, 1917.

Roussel, B. *Martin Bucer, lecteur de l'Epitre aux Romains.* Theol. diss. (typescript). Vols 1–2. Strasbourg, 1970.

Smits,L. *Saint Augustin dans l'œuvre de Jean Calvin.* Vols. 1–2. Assen, 1956–58.

Spruyt, J.B. *Wessel Gansfort and Cornelis Hoen's Epistola Christiana: "The Ring as a Pledge of My Love."* In *Wessel Gansfort (1419–1489)*, 122–41.

Wessel Gansfort. Life and Writings by Edward Waite Miller D.D. *Principal Works.* Trans. Jared Waterbury Scudder, M.A. In two Volumes. New York and London, 1917.

Wessel Gansfort (1419–1489) and Northern Humanism. Ed. F. Akkerman, G. C., Huisman and A. J. Vanderjagt. Leiden, New York, Cologne, 1993.

Biblical Index

Biblical Index

Name Index